RIGHT SEAT, RIGHT TABLE

An Outsider's Guide to Securing the Ideal Board Role

PAUL SMITH

A note on the following testimonials: It's commonplace in books like mine to include testimonials from people with some serious credentials. And, whilst I've done just that (with the likes of Jane Goodall and Cassandra Kelly), I have also included others within the Future Directors community who represent my likely readers. This includes program alumni, guest speakers and partners.

Since 1991, I have worked with young people in over 70 countries. Once they understand the problems, once we listen to their voices, once we empower them to act, their energy and determination is amazing. They are our greatest hope for the future. We must encourage them to believe in themselves and grow into leaders in their chosen way of life. This includes a position in the boardroom. My advice to anyone reading Paul's much-needed book is, "never give up". Changing the world takes persistence, passion and purpose, as well as a belief in yourself.

—Jane Goodall PhD, DBE

Founder, the Jane Goodall Institute and UN Messenger of Peace

Finally, a book that answers not only the 'how-to' of getting a board seat but asks the reader to truly understand why they would bother taking on the responsibility that follows and what kind of legacy they want to leave. The world is craving leadership at every level. If you want to be tomorrow's leader, please read Right Seat, Right Table.

—Cassandra Kelly

Tech Entrepreneur, Board Director, Adviser & Speaker
2017 Top 10 Chair in Australia
2015 US Director to Watch
Future Directors Program Speaker

It should concern all shareholders and stakeholders that the pool of director talent is relatively small, reinforcing the status quo and the unconscious biases of what a boardroom should look like. If we are to expect increased impact and returns from society's organizations, then we must also increase the size and diversity of the director talent pool to drive such change.

As an educator, mentor and thought leader, Paul Smith has not only built an impressive track record of developing and placing young and diverse people on boards, he is seeking to solve this problem.

My experience with the Future Directors Institute is that an abundance of talent and diversity exists outside the existing director pool, comparing favorably to the thousands of directors I have worked with over my career in the governance of public and private organizations. Many people could be fantastic directors but are not aware of the opportunity to contribute and how to pursue such a career. Right Seat, Right Table is a catalyst to inspire change.

—Aaron Bertinetti
Senior Vice President, Glass Lewis
Future Directors Alumni

Direct, practical, no-nonsense guide for directors from a man determined to impart the responsibility to contribute. This is indeed a roadmap for all of us, offering us great insight and challenging our EQ and IQ. It will fire your ambition to be the best director you can be and how to go from good to great!

Maria Atkinson AM
Global Non-Executive Director
Future Directors Program Speaker

Boards disproportionately impact the shape of our society and there is no more important topic worth addressing that the diversity and inclusion in the boardroom of today's businesses. Paul's insights from his own experiences and from the great work of Future Directors Institute is proof that there is a hunger from talented and heart-centered individuals who want to make a difference from the boardroom and enable a future worth committing to. Right Seat, Right Table demystifies how to obtain a board position and affect the change that our society is crying out for, let alone our businesses. The values and vision that Paul highlights is both inspiring and practical. If you are a passionate person who believes that the world needs your unique experience and talent, then becoming a board member is one of the best ways to affect change.

—Constantine Georgiou

Co-Founder, The Founder Lab
Future Directors Program Speaker

Put simply, Paul is the reason I have a boardroom career. He helped me understand my unique value and gave me the courage to seek (and achieve) my first non-executive board role at the age of 29. Without Future Directors, I would have had no idea where to start. As a media professional, I wasn't sure I "fit the mould" or had anything to offer. But Paul helped me see the opposite was true and now I'm deputy chair of a major not-for-profit. With this book, a board career might not be as far out of reach as you think.

—Hannah Stenning

Media Professional and Non-Executive Director, Delta Society
Future Directors Alumni

Paul is a pioneer in championing much needed change in boardrooms across Australia and the world. His passion and advocacy for greater diversity on boards is bringing to the fore important questions on governance, paving the way for breaking the board director stereotype, and reshaping the role of boards in our organizations.

—Elizabeth Briggs

General Counsel and Company Secretary, ClearView Wealth
Future Directors Alumni & Program Speaker

Right Seat, Right Table provides a simple yet inspiring formula for any new director seeking to get into the boardroom. I've been fortunate to serve on boards with some amazing younger members and have witnessed first-hand the benefits of their passion, instincts and unique perspectives. A career in governance is a step closer thanks to Paul's book.

—Alison Rowe

Experienced Chair and CEO
Future Directors Program Speaker

Paul's intellect, ethic, sharp wit, drive and capacity to take on multiple global projects at one time inspire me... and makes me a little envious. He is a force!

—Simon Duffy

Director, Wildlife Conservation and Science, Taronga Conservation Society
Future Directors Program Speaker

Right Seat, Right Table offers the single-most practical guide to the contemporary boardroom. Drawing on his wealth of experience, Paul mentors you to become the influencer in the boardroom, setting the tone and powering ahead of trends.

While centred around building core skills and knowledge necessary for effective performance, the importance of social responsibility, cultivating and leveraging the right relationships, and diverse board recruitment emerge as potent overarching themes.

Paul's integration of hard and soft skills will see you developing a unique leadership identity with equal parts compassion, strategic agility, and long term resilience. Regardless of where you're starting out on your pathway to your ideal board, Right Seat, Right Table takes you through how to get informed, connect career with purpose, bust a myth (or ten) and back yourself."

—Zara Bending

Non-Executive Director, the Jane Goodall Institute Australia

I have a tremendous amount of respect for Paul, what he has achieved, and the positive impact his work has had. However, I think it is about time he finds a new favourite case study, as it seems he uses my story on a near daily basis! Humour aside, I love this book, it is overflowing with inspiring case studies and easy to follow guidance. I recommend it to anyone who is aspiring board director, regardless of age or experience, as it is the practical handbook to changing the world, one directorship at a time!

—Parrys Raines "Climate Girl"

Board Member, Future Business Council
Future Directors Alumni & Program Speaker

Paul is an exceedingly passionate advocate for diversity on boards and leadership teams. His passion stems from the belief that a lack of diversity stifles creative innovation, new world problems are not usually solved by old world solutions. Through establishing Future Directors, Paul's taking a practical approach to changing the status quo, by giving people from a range of diverse age groups and professional backgrounds a roadmap to identifying their board career goals and how to achieve them. This book is a great first step to planning that journey and kick-starting a board career.

—Gaya Byrne

Non-Executive Director, The Royal Women's Hospital Foundation
Future Directors Alumni & Program Speaker

Paul's book on securing a board position is a simple and inspiring read for those who dare to dream of a better world, with more diversity and better governance. There is plenty of grounded advice and ways to think about what one's natural talents and unique attributes are. And his constant tip—remember board members are human too and our job as future directors is to have confidence and speak up without fear or favor.

—Monica Richter

Economist and Social Ecologist
Future Directors Alumni

Right Seat, Right Table is an insightful and compelling journey into the boardroom. Drawing on wisdom gained from his expansive career across the corporate and nonprofit sectors, Paul delivers a captivating guide for anybody considering taking a seat in the boardroom and exploring a purposeful and meaningful career. His book offers a powerful strategy to propel a career in the boardroom while challenging readers to embrace diversity and inclusion and serve others first and yourself second.

—Natalie Kyriacou OAM
CEO, My Green World

If you are called to make a difference in the boardroom, then Paul's book is your blueprint. Creating more conscious, sustainable organizations is Paul's mantra and he has packaged all his learnings and insights into an honest, easy to read account of the journey to the boardroom. Paul's authenticity and integrity are great guides to the messiness of leadership and the traits necessary to help organizations navigate today's complexity and ambiguity. This book is a gift that will support you to influence and impact the organizations and causes that call you so that together we can create a more conscious, sustainable world.

—Bridget Armstrong
Founder, Art of Change

For many of us, we have preconceived ideas as to what a board role requires and, too often, why we don't satisfy those requirements. Paul is passionate about focussing on the needs you do fill. He helps you ask the questions: "What do I want to do?" "What am I good at?" and "How do I apply what I'm good at to what I want to do?" And, from that, he has created the perfect starting point for a board journey.

—Jeremy Urbach
Director, Jameson Capital and State Council Member, Motor Neuron Disease Association of Victoria
Future Directors Alumni & Program Speaker

Right Seat, Right Table is a compelling summary of everything Paul Smith has built at the Future Directors Institute. It is passionately supportive of the enormous social and economic benefits of diversity and inclusion as well as entirely practical about the ways and means to take the step to participate as a Future Director. It's a must read for not only aspiring board directors, but for those chairs and boards who are responsible for recruiting positive influencers for the future of their company and society.

—Michelle Vanzella
Experienced Board Director and Start-up Advisor
Future Directors Program Speaker

As an early graduate of the Future Directors Institute, Paul's guidance and insights helped accelerate my board director journey and turn my aspiration into a reality with the right seat at the right table. Now with his must-read book, he brings together cutting-edge insights, advice and first-hand experiences as an experienced chair, board director, businessman and mentor and delivers them in this personable, practical and easy to read book. Right Seat, Right Table brings a fresh perspective on corporate governance, how to secure a board role and the skills needed to succeed and make an impact. It's a must read whether you're an aspiring or highly experienced board director.

—Jacquie Fegent-McGeachie

Chairman, Business Council for Sustainable Development Australia
Founder & CEO, Sustainovate
Future Directors Alumni & Program Speaker

Throughout my career, the interactions I'd had with the boards of large organizations left me alternately bored or terrified; board members or board committees who are either so risk-averse they were paralysed or mistakenly confident that they sought no input from me, other than to act as instructed. As I got older I realised that not only did boards need to change if they were to succeed in the future, but that I was going to have to be part of that change.

It's no small thing for a scruffy nerd in jeans and t-shirt to pitch themselves as a non-executive director, especially a business school drop-out with a background as an early-stage tech start-up founder and angel investor. Working with Paul and the Future Directors Institute helped me recognise my strengths and experience, learn the lingo, and draft a plan for what kind of boards to pitch to and how to go about it.

Thanks to them, I'm serving as a director and have half a clue about what I'm doing. My long-term goal (to be the tech innovation expert on an Australian ASX100 board) will happen when it happens. In the meantime, my reputation as an effective director is growing.

Paul's book distils so much of what he and Future Directors teach in their workshops and programs that I highly recommend you read it if you aspire to break into the boardroom.

—Alan Jones

Entrepreneur in Residence, muru-D, Tech Investor
Future Directors Alumni & Program Speaker

Paul's advice about making it into the boardroom—and most importantly, having influence and impact when you get there—is practical and priceless. The CONNECT methodology that provides the framework for his book has worked for me, and I have seen it work for others. Follow it and not only will it help you find the ideal board role; you will also have a deeper understanding of what you have to offer and how you can make a difference.

—Peter O'Sullivan

National Head of People & Culture, BDO Australia
Non-Executive Director, Queensland Doctors' Health Programme
Future Directors Alumni

I've often wondered what it would take for business to wake up and realize the benefits of boardroom diversity, particularly when it comes to age, gender and skillset. One of the unstoppable forces in creating better boardrooms for a better world is Paul Smith. He is at the frontline of helping young(er) people find their feet in a world that was previously seemingly inaccessible for people like me—the boardroom. With immense passion, wit and articulation, he demystifies the boardroom archetype and offers some practical advice and home truths to help you break into your first board role.

—Nadia Woodhouse
Global Center for Board Matters, Ernst Young
Future Directors Program Speaker

Increasingly, many people want to join a board so they can contribute and help change our world for the better. But it's a big leap to make it happen - one that can feel daunting. Paul provides a practical blueprint for translating that aspiration into reality, while also asking the right questions to know whether the director path is a good fit. If you're keen to explore whether the boardroom is the place for you to have an impact, this is the book for you.

—Anna Byrne
Partner, NeuroPower Group
Board Director at the age of 17!

RIGHT SEAT, RIGHT TABLE

An Outsider's Guide to
Securing the Ideal Board Role

PAUL SMITH

Profits from the sale of the book are donated in a selection of Paul's favorite causes around the world.

First published in 2019 by Future Directors Institute

hello@futuredirectors.com | www.futuredirectors.com

A catalogue record for this book is available from the National Library of New Zealand.

ISBN: 978-0-473-46454-7 (Softcover version)
ISBN: 978-0-473-46455-4 (eBook version)
ISBN: 978-0-473-46456-1 (PDF version)

CONTENTS

ACKNOWLEDGEMENTS

To you, thank you for taking the time to read a book, any book! And thank you even more for choosing to invest your time and energy in *my* book. I truly hope you gain valuable insights that justify your investment.

To my family, especially Millie and Ollie: Thank you for being patient. For years, you've listened to my pain, my joy, my whining, and my guilt for not writing this book sooner! Without your love and support, this book would never have been written.

To my team and co-founder Warwick: It's been a long road and we've had our ups and downs, but this book is as much a celebration of what we've achieved, as it is a look to the future.

To my editorial and creative team, Akiko, Sandra, Kathryn, Najdan and Andrija: Without your encouragement, experience, flair, and insight, this would have never come to pass. You have been a revelation. A huge thank you also to book-writing guru and international author, Andrew Griffiths, for your sage wisdom when I'd hit a wall.

Finally, to our community: You continue to amaze and inspire me. Without you, there would be no book, no business, no change. Thank you.

YOUR IDEAL BOARD ROLE

Stepping into a boardroom can be an intimidating experience, even if you're a seasoned executive from a large publicly listed company. For the outsider, it can be difficult to know what's expected of you and how to go about getting into the boardroom—not just any boardroom, but the one that best matches your value and your values and represents your passions, your interests, and the stakeholders you wish to serve. This is what I mean by "ideal". It's whatever suits you—and the board. It's a balance, a match, and a meeting of needs.

An ideal board role will be different for each person. It could be on what I'd call a traditional governance board, with all the legal responsibilities that come with that. Or it could be on an advisory board or subcommittee that comes with other non-legal responsibilities. It could involve a full-time commitment as a professional director with a portfolio or, more likely, a part-time responsibility along with your day job. It might be a paid role with a company in a sector that interests you or a voluntary position on a charitable board of trustees for a cause that is close to your heart.

Tip: *Ideal = a balance of your passions, interests, and skills and the needs of the boardroom that best matches your value and values.*

This book is designed to help you develop a clear strategy for accelerating your journey to these ideal board roles. You might only be researching what the boardroom and being a director are all about, or you might be ready to step into your first board role. Wherever you are in the process, remember that it's better to know now what you'll need than to wait until you think you are ready.

This book is designed for the outsider. If you are not already inside the boardroom or don't fit the traditional mold, then you'll find this book especially helpful. It is based on the combined wisdom drawn from numerous board journeys made by me and by hundreds of people just like you. I've tried to make this roadmap as simple and easy to follow as possible, but I encourage you to read the entire book first, and then return to the parts that require key practical actions (highlighted at the end of specific chapters).

In the book, I cover:

Basics of the boardroom and being a non-executive director

» Top reasons people want to become directors

» Myths surrounding the boardroom

» CONNECT: our proven methodology for finding your ideal board roles

» Case studies from our community that bring our method to life and will inspire and empower you on your boardroom journey

» Mistakes to avoid as you attempt to find and secure your ideal board role

» Common challenges faced by new directors and how to overcome them

» Finally, key attributes and skills that will make you an effective, successful, and influential director in any boardroom—and, perhaps, a Future Director!

Are you ready? Let's do this!

But first....

WHERE IT BEGAN, AND WHERE WE'RE GOING

At the Future Directors Institute, we aim to nurture a diverse next generation of talent for the boardroom. Our belief is that diversity extends far beyond gender, age, and cultural background to skills, thought processes, personal experiences, and individual perspectives.

The boardroom of any entity, be it a large corporation, nonprofit, startup, school, or community organization, has a critical influence on a wide range of stakeholders and, therefore, can be a conduit for progress and change. Decisions made in the boardroom about strategic direction, risk management, workplace culture, products, and services impact not just customers and employees but the wider community, society, and the often-overlooked environment. The extent of that impact depends on the scope and influence of the organization. But even the most local organization can have an effect that ripples out beyond its stakeholders.

Many years ago, I recognized the potential for boardrooms to better address and solve individual, organizational, and societal challenges. I also recognized that, in many boardrooms, the status quo was stagnating innovation and collaboration and was preventing businesses from evolving into forces for positive and inclusive progress.

My conclusion: We need more "outsiders" in the boardroom, people with new skills and from different backgrounds. We need more diversity and inclusion.

I first publicly pitched the idea of Future Directors at a conference in front of hundreds of young professionals and impact investors. The name of the conference was "Nexus" and my ideas and reasoning resonated with more people than I expected. From there I was inspired to gather like-minded people together to examine how to address this issue.

Through these first initial steps and discussions, I also met my (eventual) co-founder Warwick Peel. Together, we established Future Directors (initially called XY on Boards). We made it our mission to cultivate a new level of diversity and inclusion in boardrooms by building a strong, supportive community of people who aspire to be catalysts for meaningful change.

Our aim was to enable these change makers to be successful in gaining positions in the boardrooms where they could make the greatest impact and then, over time, to help them influence the change that is needed.

Consider your commitment
Own your unique value
Nail your assets
Network your value
Execute the right plan
Conduct your due diligence
Thrive in the boardroom

Over the past several years, we have helped hundreds of diverse professionals to kick-start or accelerate their non-executive boardroom careers using our CONNECT method, workshops, online courses, and award-winning programs. Our specialty is helping the younger professional, generally aged 25 to 45. But we do not discriminate and we welcome anyone who wants to make a difference in the boardroom. For example, we've helped baby boomers seeking to transition to professional directorship. As you'll discover, the route to the boardroom is difficult if you don't know what you are doing.

Whether you're simply curious or you're a brand new, emerging, or experienced board director, there will always be a place in the Future Directors Institute for fresh thinkers and doers who share our vision of a better world led by better boards. This is what excites us: the energy, the purpose, and the motivations of our growing community.

Why and how did the Future Directors Institute begin?

The concept came to me 15 years ago when I was first exposed to the boardroom. In my late 20s, I was working in London on a project with a large global investment company and dealing closely with the company board. My first impression of that board fit the stereotypical image that most of us have: all white, all male, and all older than the average professional.

Let me be clear from the outset. There is nothing wrong with being an older white male. (I'm not that far from being one myself.) The problem, in my opinion, is that they hold too many leadership and board positions, which makes boardrooms too homogenous in thought and too masculine in nature. What's lost are the different perspectives and skills that are brought by non-typical board directors (although this is not to say that gender, age, or cultural diversity necessarily guarantee a different or better boardroom culture).

If you look at some stereotypes that often make traditional boardrooms nervous about outsider candidates, you'll see that those "weaknesses" can actually create a better and more balanced board. Young directors are often dismissed as inexperienced, rash, or overconfident. But they bring fresh ideas and knowledge, such as digital savvy. Women are often thought as too indecisive and lacking the leadership skills to be effective board directors. In actuality, many women are more collaborative as decision makers, and it's rare to find a group of men that consistently makes well-considered decisions.

It's important to remember that, whether young, old, male, or female, we are not our stereotypes. So what makes the real difference is what the individual brings and how boards are recruited.

Now, back to my first boardroom encounter. The board in question was predominantly composed of legal and finance professionals. I found it peculiar that this group was making strategic decisions about the company's global rebranding, something of which they had little knowledge or experience.

The group's homogeneity seemed normal and unchallenged, and diversity among the directors didn't seem to be an option. But the experience planted a question in my mind that would lie dormant for the next decade: Why wasn't there more diversity among board members when their decisions impact such a broad spectrum of people?

After I moved to Australia in search of a bit of sunshine, I embarked on a journey of personal development. I lacked direction, an agenda of my own, and, frankly, a reason for being. I wanted to *do* something, and I tried to figure out what that might be. This period of self-discovery taught me more about what I was good at *and* what the world needed more of. I started to see business not just as a vehicle for profit and employment but also as a vehicle for socially responsible influence and change. I joined groups advocating for impact investment, conscious capitalism, social enterprise, and benefit corporations.

However, even within these communities, I continued to see an element of disconnect between what the world needs and how businesses were being led. In so many organizations, it was still profit above all else. But I also saw that there were businesses that were driven by more than profit alone—by doing good work, treating employees well, and providing customers with great products and services— and they were performing better. And that begged the question: Were they governed better?

In my early thirties, I had the chance to join my first board, a purely fortuitous opportunity (so I thought). While I was attending a company-sponsored event, the organizer

I'd been working closely with recognized my strategic potential and mentioned that I would be a great fit for that organization's board. After an introduction to the CEO and interviews with the chair and other directors, I was offered a positon and accepted it.

I soon noticed that my new board had ample passion but lacked a coherent strategy. It also had (in my opinion) low governance standards. After listening to them and assessing things over the first few months, I communicated my misgivings and ideas to the chair. To her credit and the board's credit, they recognized the need for refreshed leadership, innovative thinking, and new blood. Within a year, I was elected to the position of board chair and set about bringing new people into the organization to deliver what was missing.

As my tenure on that board continued, I kept coming back to my early question: Where was the diversity and inclusion? And where was the connection to the wider, real world? The board's intentions were good and the group was smart and dedicated, but it was becoming difficult to ignore that we were standing on shaky ground. I began to wonder whether the lack of clarity and direction was specific to this board or whether this was the general status quo.

Ever curious, feeling disruptive, and inspired to assist with change wherever I could, I began investigating more of the governance world. As I spoke to other directors, peers, and colleagues, I came to realize that rudderless, disconnected boards were common.

The notion of Future Directors ultimately came to me during yet another board presentation, to a board I was working with at the time. The chairman, who had recently discovered and was utterly enamored with social media, effused endlessly about it and monopolized most of the meeting. Maybe this seems minor, but I was so angry that this board was wasting time on ego and vanity.

That moment crystallized my observations that boardroom culture had become shallow and disconnected and was in desperate need of an overhaul. My own beliefs and philosophies were evolving around both my own purpose and what was needed in the world. I saw more clearly a formula for businesses, indeed all organizations, that could inspire change from within. As all these ideas and thoughts converged, the blueprint for Future Directors was born.

Once I began exploring this opportunity, I found many other board directors who were equally discouraged by this status quo: the lack of diversity, inclusion, and connection to the real world. They too could see that the kind of pioneering change they envisioned had to start in the boardroom.

I have an innate ability to see potential in people. I thrive on helping them figure out where they want to be and how they can get there. How better to help steer meaningful change than by cultivating a group of people who have the potential and the motivation to do so?

When I first set up Future Directors with Warwick Peel in 2015, one of our main goals was to create a community where like-minded individuals could be assisted in their pursuit of a board role. Our intention was to encourage diversification of the boardroom, and over the next few decades, successfully disrupt its status quo, introduce fresh thinking and new blood, and evolve the boardroom into a place of innovation and societal progress. Although we were starting in Australia, we knew our project had to be international. We had and still have very international aspirations and are working on projects and opportunities in Asia and North America. The plan is to introduce the concept of Future Directors to all parts of the world in partnership with businesses and communities who share our vision that the boardroom can be, and is, a conduit for change.

In realizing this vision, our main ambition is to accelerate the inclusion of outsiders in the boardroom and to help shape boards whose work benefits all, rather than a single set of stakeholders. We want to see this at all levels and across all types of organizations, not just corporate boards. Nonprofits are not exempt from the need for change. This might seem like an uphill journey, especially given our human instinct to resist change, but it's one that drives me forward every day.

There are people in every community who are working daily toward making a difference, even on a small scale. These are the people that the Future Directors Institute is looking for. We want to continue building a community of support and understanding that will help these people advance not only in their personal careers but in roles on a broader scale too.

What is a Future Director?

In your journey into and through the boardroom, we try to help you move toward becoming what we call a "Future Director", a concept I explain below. This journey starts with your aspirations, and this book covers the steps you need to take to progress from Aspiring to Developing Director.

Let's first go over how we define these stages.

Aspiring Director: You are starting out on your boardroom journey, and you are developing your skills, networks, and credibility. Perhaps you have been inspired by an Developing or Future Director, someone who started at a young age and shares your values. Your motivations are a combination of developing new skills and networks, giving back, and making a difference. Money can play a part, but it's not your primary motivator.

Developing Director: You are relatively new to the boardroom and have made it there within the past few years. You are probably experiencing some challenges, but you can already see the opportunities to influence and deepen the impact you are making, especially because you bring something unique to the group.

Future Director: You are the influencer in the boardroom. You are driven by a deeper purpose and can motivate others to better express their ideas and be more effective. Others look to you for your opinion and guidance. On a personal level, you have discovered your natural talents and turned them into your core strengths. You earn more money, have more fun, and attract more opportunity. You are highly credible and visible in the world of governance because your diverse perspectives, new ideas, and collaborative mindset bring value. You are ethical, responsible, and proactive. You are highly motivated to keep growing your skills and your ability to shape the future from the boardroom, and indeed, to shape the boardroom for the future.

Would you like to become a Future Director? This book is an invitation to take the first step in that journey: finding and securing your ideal board role. I also give you some insight into what it takes to move from being an Developing Director to a Future Director.

PART I

An Introduction To The Boardroom

CHAPTER 1

BOARDROOM BASICS

What is a board director anyway?

Before you start this journey, it's important that you know what will be expected of you as a director. Because the topic has been covered extensively elsewhere, including in our training programs at the Future Directors Institute, I won't go into too much detail here. But I'll give you enough so you'll know what you're getting into.

There are two types of directors on a board. Executive directors are employees of the company or organization and are responsible for management and operations. Non-executive directors have no responsibilities for the company or the organization's operations, but they do play a key role in its strategic direction, risk management, and financial stability.

We are going to focus on becoming a non-executive director. Depending on the type of entity being served, a board director may be known by different names: trustee, member, councilor, and governor are a few common titles.

For the purposes of this book, we'll use the term "director" to encompass all similar roles, no matter what the naming convention is.

The strategies and methods illustrated in this book will work for you regardless of the type of board you wish to join. People following these strategies and methods have secured paid roles on listed company boards as well as volunteer roles with small nonprofits. They've become advisors to startups and joined school boards and philanthropic foundations.

Why do boards exist, and what do they do?

Boards, or governing bodies, have been around for thousands of years. The Greeks and Romans had governing groups creating their laws and defining the direction of civil society and the economy. More recently, entities such as the British East India Trading Company in the 17th century gave rise to today's corporate board. These company boards were established to act on behalf of the owners and to be responsible for their financial interests. It was and still is all about *trust*, hence the term "trustee".

Today, the typical duties of a board of directors include:

1. **Selecting,** appointing, supporting, evaluating, removing, and remunerating the manager of the organization. There are many titles for 'manager'. Typically, the manager is the CEO, the executive director, or the president.

2. **Providing** strategic direction for the organization. The board has a strategic function in deciding the purpose, vision, mission, and goals of the organization, most commonly in collaboration with management.

3. **Establishing** a policy-based governance system. Each organization is regulated by the government and oversight bodies, such as stock exchanges, but the board has a responsibility to develop the policies, rules, and frameworks for how the organization will function, guiding not just the board's own actions but the actions of management.

4. **Governing** the relationship with the CEO and establishing systems for their interactions, including setting objectives, measuring performance, and reporting needs. Typically, board members meet with each other and key members of management on a regular basis, and the board is kept informed of what's going on in the interim through different forms of communication.

5. **Exercising** fiduciary duty to protect the financial interests of owners or members. These might include physical assets, intellectual property, and the human capital (employees). The board is responsible for ensuring that adequate financial resources are available for the organization to conduct its business and achieve its strategic objectives.

6. Monitoring and auditing the organization. The board is responsible for the audit process, hires the auditor, and ensures the audit is done in a timely manner each year.

Currently, there are no universally recognized or observed governance standards. Many groups have their own set of policies and standards that impact the extent to which the above duties are managed by the board or by management.

Are there different types of boards?

"All boards are the same, and all boards are different."

This is the book's first lesson, and in my opinion, one of its most fundamental lessons.

What do I mean by this? The only thing common to all boards is that they are a group of human beings. Therefore, by extension, they are also all different because each of us is unique, and the boardroom is a unique combination of personalities, experiences, ages, genders, backgrounds, skills, biases, and gaps.

Most organizations within the private, nonprofit, and public sectors have some type of governance body, but that body can vary significantly in size, structure, and function. In general, the processes and the level of integrity and ethical judgment are (or should be) the same, regardless of the type of board. However, boards operate slightly differently in each sector.

Private and corporate sector: This sector is largely profit-driven, and governance roles with these organizations are often (but not always) remunerated. The sector covers a broad range of organizations from publicly listed companies to small businesses and family-owned operations. It also includes the increasingly popular sectors of startups, B corps, and social enterprise, whose companies may not be solely profit-motivated.

Board appointments are usually made by owners (or voted on by shareholders), but the board of directors leads the process. The appointment process is highly competitive, particularly for businesses that are national in scale or publicly listed on a stock exchange.

Nonprofit sector: These boards support organizations that may serve the community. They cover many sectors, including human and community services, sports and recreation, culture and arts, environment, and heritage, to name a few. Appointments to a nonprofit board are usually endorsed by the membership at an annual general meeting or by election.

Being a board member of a nonprofit organization can be challenging, but it is a good entry point for learning about governance. As most positions are unpaid, board members are generally motivated by their desire to give back. Board roles for nonprofits can be far more hands-on than roles on corporate boards.

Public (or government) sector: The stakeholders for these boards are generally taxpayers and citizens (and their government representatives), so public sector boards are driven by considerations of the public interest.

These boards must work within a legal framework. Board members are often remunerated, but generally at lower levels than board members of large corporations. The boards can be political and very process-driven, although they are generally concerned about positive efficacy.

Appointments are usually made by government officials.

Are there different roles in the boardroom?

Most boards include a group of office holders. These generally comprise at least a chair (also known as chairperson, chairman, or chairwoman), deputy chair, treasurer, and secretary, whose roles are described below. Many boards also have subcommittees that focus on particular issues, such as audit, risk, finance, recruitment, and fundraising. Directors are often asked to sit on one or more board committees.

Each of the roles below can be either executive or non-executive. It depends on the structure and ownership of the organization.

Chair: The chair leads the board and serves as its main spokesperson. The chair manages board meetings and ensures that the discussion remains focused and members observe meeting rules. Some chairs are also given an additional casting vote to use when votes on the board are evenly divided. With most boards, the chair acts as the intermediary between the board and the CEO. The relationship between the CEO and chair is vital. A strong bond between them will enhance the effectiveness of any board.

Deputy Chair: Many boards appoint a deputy chair to support the chair and to fill in when the chair is absent. The deputy chair is also expected to play a major role in board leadership.

Treasurer: The treasurer is responsible for the integrity of the financials. They monitor the organization's financial position and keep other board members informed of financial matters. In many companies, this is an executive role and the responsibility of the chief financial officer.

Secretary: Often known as company secretary (whether nonprofit or corporate), the person in this role ensures that an organization complies with its legal and regulatory obligations and that decisions made by the board of directors are implemented. In many companies, this is also an executive role because of its complexity.

Administrative Support: A board can be provided with administrative support through the organization's management structure or as a board role. They may be known as a secretary or executive officer. This role is responsible for tasks such as maintaining records and preparing and distributing meeting agendas and minutes.

Is "Chairman" a sexist term?

It may seem trivial to some, but I do not believe in using the term "Chairman", even if the role is filled by a man. Some argue that it's now a gender-neutral term, like "human", and it's commonplace for men and women to go by "Chairman". But I would argue it's just as gender specific as "Chairwoman", and I haven't known any man to adopt "Chairwoman" as his title, have you? "Chairperson" is another increasingly used term, but it's just too much of a mouthful. So, I'm sticking with "Chair".

Why am I so passionate about this? It's about the message the choice sends. Whether intended or not, for some people, "Chairman" tells them this is a male role. In fact, good chairs are guides who nurture boardroom cultures and build key relationships. These are distinctly *female* traits.

If you think I'm being too politically correct, then you're not going to like Future Directors at all! Being PC is about doing right by others. It's about social justice, equality of opportunity, compassion, and above all, respect. Indifference, apathy, and outright discrimination have no place among Future Directors.

There you are. Rant over. On with the book.

CHAPTER 2

MOTIVATIONS AND MYTHS

What motivates people to be board directors?

One question we ask all aspiring directors is, "Why do you want to be a board director?" Knowing your motivation is a key step to starting your board career journey and to becoming a more experienced and capable leader.

If you are reading this book, you probably have a reason for pursuing a board role. But, if you've never given it much thought, this would be a good time to start asking yourself that question. And if you don't know where to begin, take a look at the list below. It shows you the top five reasons members of our community choose to be non-executive board directors.

This list is presented in reverse order of importance to our community:

> **Tip:** *What is motivating you into the boardroom? Remember, this is your journey, and what is right for someone else might not be right for you.*

Increased earnings: Money is rarely the primary motivator when it comes to joining a board. Compensation for board roles is not especially large, and most aspiring directors understand from the outset that they won't be earning extravagant salaries.

While your first board role won't necessarily be unpaid, nonprofit boards (which are mostly volunteer) outnumber commercial boards by a factor of 10. Corporate boards can also be a notoriously tight club to get into, especially if you're an outsider and deemed inexperienced.

Although many people work their way up from an unpaid board role to a paid one, don't let anyone convince you that the only way to start a board career is on a nonprofit volunteer board. Not everyone is on the same journey as you. In fact, 1 in 10 of our Future Directors Institute community accepted a paid board role after our program. For most of the them, this was their first governance role, and given that they are, on average, in their mid-thirties, that's very impressive!

Building a portfolio career: If you are a younger professional, then it's likely you are used to a different sort of economy than your mature counterparts. (In the boardroom, "younger" means under 40 or even under 50, according to PwC's Annual Global Director Survey.)

In the past, people would get an education, start a career, and remain in that career for the rest of their lives. It's increasingly common to move from job to job and career to career, or even to take on a number of different jobs at once. This is known as a portfolio career. Many younger professionals have realized that a board role can help them to build an impressive portfolio, especially if they get started early.

Becoming a better leader and learning new skills: You can learn many priceless skills in the boardroom, including everything from leadership to finance, governance to strategy, and decision-making to group dynamics. This sort of experience can teach you so much about yourself and others. It can also enhance your existing skills and enable you to perform better both in and out of the boardroom.

Outsiders—such as younger directors—who adopt this learning attitude also recognize that they bring a different set of skills and knowledge to the boardroom than the older members. This multigenerational diversity and inclusion can be endlessly beneficial on both an individual and an organizational level. Joining a board helps you learn from the people around you. It also gives you the opportunity to share your knowledge and experiences with those same people. This sort of learning and exposure can be especially meaningful if you want to align yourself with an organization and a mission that are impactful and sustainable.

This is one part of giving back.

Giving back: There is a commonly held belief of boardrooms as purely corporate environments with no real heart or soul. This couldn't be further from the truth. The desire to serve others is a significant driving force behind many people's decision to become a board director. These people have realized what they're passionate about and how they can contribute.

Some people choose to support causes through monetary contributions (i.e. philanthropy). For those who choose to serve on boards, their support comes in the form of their skills, expertise, and time—which can be worth just as much as any dollar amount. In many instances, these things are even more valuable. And board directors are starting to understand this.

Making a difference: Since we started Future Directors Institute, we've spoken to hundreds of professionals about their reasons for joining a board. Making a difference is the number one reason they gave and still give. Not everyone has aspirations for global change, but almost everyone wants to positively influence or change some aspect of their world. For professional leaders, joining a board is a very effective step toward doing so.

Thanks to advances in the media and sharing technology, we are more aware of what's really going on in our world. We know about every inspiring and demoralizing event as it's happening, and it's this knowledge that motivates so many of us to influence change.

Younger professionals care about many things, including social justice, inequality, technological innovation, and climate change, and those concerns are often inherently intertwined. While these issues are not new, younger professionals have an attitude about them that is new. They don't expect other people to solve these problems on their behalf. Instead, they wonder, "Why wait for them to make a difference? Why can't I start doing it today?" Therefore, they're choosing to shape their own future, and they understand that the right board role can be pivotal in this.

The best board roles satisfy all of these motivations and reward you in ways that you might not anticipate.

Myth Busters: The Boardroom Edition

When it comes to boardrooms, there is plenty of myth and conjecture—especially for those who have never been exposed to boardrooms before. I believe that, because of these misconceptions, there are many professionals who would be great in a board position but haven't even considered it as a possibility for themselves.

At Future Directors Institute, one of our main goals is helping people to get past the obstacle of stereotypes and realize what they have to contribute. Here are the top three boardroom myths that most would-be directors tend to believe and why they're just not true:

"I don't have the right skills or experience": The popular perception is that boardrooms are only for high-flying corporate types at their peak of ability and experience, as this is how boards are portrayed in the media. This is also not far from their traditional character.

Fortunately, the better boards have started to realize the importance of attracting directors with diverse experiences and skills. This slow revolution will help to dispel the misconception that only lawyers, accountants, and C-suite executives can be board directors.

> **Tip:** *Don't let anyone tell you you're not ready to be a board director! Your readiness starts with your commitment to making it happen. It also depends on having appropriate expectations of when this is possible for you and which boards might need someone just like you.*

There is no single template for a board director, as each board has different needs. Yes, they might require lawyers, finance professionals, and people with C-suite experience, but that might not be all they need. For example, many corporate boards are seeking people with HR experience in order to help them effectively navigate workplace culture, which is currently a major (and relatively new) focus of many boardrooms. In addition, many organizations need directors with knowledge and experience in digital marketing, social media, and fundraising. Our alumni community includes nearly every type of white-collar profession you can think of, including entrepreneurs, consultants, investment analysts, marketers, digital experts, engineers, media and communications specialists, and even academics!

Ongoing learning and skills development are prerequisites for success in board careers. Even if you feel you don't have all the necessary skills, you can always gain more of the skills you need down the road and on the job. No matter where your experience lies, from engineering or entrepreneurialism to technology or finance, be assured that there are boards out there looking for someone with your exact experience and abilities.

"I don't look the part": Many Future Directors Institute alumni have told us that they didn't consider seeking a board position purely because they didn't think they looked the part. Most boardrooms are conservative in nature because risk identification and management are key responsibilities. This focus on risk can extend to the recruitment of directors. Boards tend to stick with who and what they know.

The general lack of diversity has discouraged people who are younger, of a different gender, race, or background from aspiring to a directorship. But these people are exactly who are needed on boards. It's widely recognized that cognitive diversity is the most important factor in a high-performing boardroom—and this key mix of skills and experience is more likely to come from people of diverse backgrounds, ages, and genders. Diversity has become necessary for today's boardroom. Organizations assume risk when their board is homogenous.

A large number of boards are becoming aware of the benefits of diversity, but it is still considered a secondary priority. According to PwC's 2018 *Annual Corporate Directors Survey*, while gender and age diversity are important to almost all boards, they rank below the main priorities for boards. These priorities include technology expertise, environmental and social governance (ESG) strategies, and shareholder activism.

Many boards simply fail to see the total value of diversity. When boards make diversity one of their highest priorities, they will be able to overcome many of the other issues they're facing and the risks they're trying to mitigate. If technology expertise is a need, the traditional board director won't have much to contribute. If shareholder activism is on an organization's radar, the board needs good strategists and professional communicators. For many boards today, professionals who don't fit the board director stereotype are often the perfect candidates.

Aspiring directors and boards share the responsibility to drive diversity. It is on your shoulders to ignore the myth and step up into the boardroom. But it's also up to boardrooms to encourage a broad spectrum of professionals to see that they have a place on a board.

Before we move on to CONNECT, our proven methodology for developing a strategy and action plan for securing your ideal board role, we'll look at the first of our many case studies. The aim is to bring these chapters to life with real-world examples of people just like you, making their board careers happen.

HANNAH STENNING:
Setting Her Sights on the Boardroom

Like many in our community, Hannah is proving to the world that you don't have to be cut from the traditional director cloth to make it as a successful non-executive board director. She is a trailblazer in the media industry: She became the first commissioning editor for Australia's biggest news website (news.com.au), where she spearheaded the organization's first Facebook live leaders' debate ahead of the 2016 Australian national election. Since turning her sights to the boardroom, she's landed a major role with a nonprofit organization that believes in improving the bond between dogs and people of all ages.

When Hannah first realized that she wanted to join a board, her first thought was that she had no clue where to start. She'd heard of all the advantages that come with being on a board. But, becoming a director seemed like a far-off prospect. She also didn't know if a boardroom would want her anyway. It wasn't until she started on her journey with us that she realized the value of what she had to offer and how to find her perfect board role.

Hannah learned that her career in media would make her an attractive proposition to many boardrooms. She also identified the industries where her experience and expertise were most applicable. Beyond that, Hannah developed the confidence in herself to approach prospective boards.

She forced herself to talk about herself and share her skill sets and career qualities with other members of the Future Directors cohort. This gave her the confidence to go out and do it.

As she continued her journey, she began putting into action everything she'd learned. She let her networks know that she was on the lookout for director positions. That's how she heard about the charity she ultimately joined. Like Hannah, the organization has big goals. So, it's no surprise that, after she approached them, Hannah was offered an interview to join their board. It was the first and only board Hannah applied to join and now she's in a position to apply her skills and experience to a cause that she loves.

PART II

What You Need To Become
A Board Director

CHAPTER 3

THE FIVE Cs OF BECOMING A NON-EXECUTIVE DIRECTOR

In the first part of the book, we covered my story and that of the Future Directors Institute, what it means to be a non-executive director, and why you might want to be a director in the first place. Hopefully, we also busted some myths about boards.

Now we get into what it takes to become a non-executive director and how you can develop a clear roadmap and action plan to win your ideal board role.

Tip: *It's easier to stand out from the crowd if you stand for something bigger than yourself. Getting the ideal board role on your terms is about your value, your commitment, your goals, and your relationships. If you want people to support you, give them something and someone amazing to support.*

What does it take to find and secure your ideal board role? You'll need the right combination of what we call the five Cs:

COMMITMENT—Know what you want and when you want it.

CONTRIBUTION—Articulate your unique contribution to the boardroom.

CREDIBILITY—Demonstrate that you would be an asset, not a risk.

COMMUNITY—It's all about who knows you and what they say about you.

CONFIDENCE—You know you can take on the challenge and secure your ideal role.

Let's delve a little deeper into the five Cs.

Commitment

Your commitment sets the tone for your journey in the boardroom. Why do you want to be a board director? We've already covered the most common reasons, so which one(s) resonate most with you? When do you want to be on a board? Who are the stakeholders you want to serve? Having clarity of focus and intent is vital. You won't get far with ambivalence: "I want to be on a board, but I don't care which one". A better place to start if you're not sure is "I want to be on a board, and I want to find out which one".

You also need to ask yourself: "Do I have the time to serve on a board?" It's worth noting that the time commitment for a board role is not uniform. Some roles, such as on advisory boards, might entail only a few hours every month; other roles could involve over 20 hours per month of meetings, preparation, events, and more; still others might require several days per week (perhaps even up to 100 hours per month). It all depends on the type of board and its needs. It's best to start by asking yourself how much time you have and then add this to your search criteria. For many boards, though, you can assume about 20 hours per month to serve as a director. You can also estimate that you'll have to commit this same amount of time to finding the role.

If you can respond positively to each of these statements, you are well on your way to commitment:

> » I can clearly articulate my reasons for wanting to be a non-executive director.
> » I know what type of board I want to be on, when, and why.
> » I have the capacity and time to commit to not only finding my ideal role but also fulfilling the role itself.

If you aren't there yet, don't worry. Just keep reading!

Contribution

If your commitment drives you, your contribution defines you. What value will you add to an organization as a non-executive director? Do you understand the underlying responsibilities of a director? Do you know what will be expected of you?

If you're young, you may not bring governance experience (i.e., years spent in the boardroom or even at a senior leadership level), but don't let that deter you. You could bring passion, diverse skills and expertise, new perspectives honed in our multifaceted and digitalized world, innovative thinking, creativity, or a technology-aware mindset. While many boards are focusing on cultivating members with digital experience, this doesn't mean you need to have technical expertise such as programming. It is enough that you were born into a world of social media, mobile devices, and apps, and that operating with this technology is second nature.

If you can respond positively to each of these statements, you are well on your way to being able to make a valuable contribution:

- » I know the roles and responsibilities of the board and its directors.

- » I know what my ideal board position needs from me and can clearly articulate why I'm the perfect candidate.

- » I am continuing to refine my unique boardroom value proposition as I develop my skills, strengths, and attributes.

Credibility

Boards are generally risk-averse groups that are reluctant to take a chance on the unknown or the outsider. Even though you and I know that boards need new blood, how can you present yourself as a potential asset, and not a risk, to a typically conservative board? This comes down to how you think, look, and act. For example, what do others say about you? Remember, people will buy what you are selling only if they know others have bought it!

What you know and who you know are important, but in the context of finding and securing your ideal board role, I always say that it's more important who knows you and what they say about you. We'll explore this in more detail in a short while.

What does it take to give the impression that you're a potentially valuable director, even if you have no formal governance experience or training? How have you positioned yourself both online and offline? Can you communicate how your skills, strengths, and experiences will serve the board, the organization, and the stakeholders?

If you can respond positively to each of these statements, you are well on your way to credibility:

> » I know how to tailor my board CV to match the needs of my target organization and to fully reflect my unique value proposition.
>
> » I think and behave like a board director, and this is demonstrated by how I present myself both online (e.g., LinkedIn, blogs, engagement) and offline (e.g., in-person networking and interviews).
>
> » Even if I have no formal board experience, I can demonstrate prior experience that is relevant to governance roles and responsibilities.

Community

They say that it takes a village to raise a child. I say the same about any leader or board director: It takes connection and community.

Boards are recruited largely via close networks, so being in the right place at the right time is the most effective way to find your ideal board role. You might think this is just about luck. It's not. It's about positioning yourself within the right community. You need to broaden your networks in the right areas. For example, if you want to be on a social enterprise board, build relationships with people and influencers in that community. Impress upon them your **commitment, contribution,** and **credibility.** If you already have some connections to this community, keep developing them. It never hurts to have deeper relationships.

Ultimately, the best way to accelerate your board career is to develop mentors and sponsors. Both need to understand what you want, why, and when. They need to know how much value you could add (because you've articulated this to them clearly). They must support your aspirations and want to help you achieve them. When sponsors hear of an opening or opportunity, they will connect you to the board or the board to you.

Trust is the ultimate currency of the boardroom. It's why boards can be so reluctant to recruit outsiders. You need to build trust with the right people who know you and want to talk about you to others.

You shouldn't go it alone. You need this village. Besides mentors and sponsors, you should be reaching out to current directors, especially in the sectors and board types that you aspire to, or even the actual boards that you wish to sit on.

Finally, surround yourself with like-minded people on a similar journey. Seek each other out for support, and hold each other to account (inside and outside the boardroom). Entrepreneurs do it. Employees do it. So why not board directors? You need a community to help you learn and develop in ways that you'll be able to succeed.

If you can respond positively to each of these statements, you are well on your way to connection:

> » I have a community that is helping me in my journey into the boardroom, including one or more mentors.

> » I am surrounded by a like-minded group of aspiring and developing directors who are supportive of what I'm trying to achieve.

> » I am continuously networking with directors and other key people of influence and am confident that all of them would act as a sponsor if the opportunity presented itself.

Confidence

Ultimately, getting in front of the people who recruit new board directors (whether it's the boards themselves or third-party recruitment agents) comes down to confidence. How confident are you that you can find the roles that are the right fit for you and for them? How confident are you that you will secure and nail the interview stage? How confident are you that you'll make the right decision if you receive an offer? (Not every board role should be accepted, as we'll look at later.)

If you can respond positively to each of these statements, you are well on your way to confidence:

» I have a clear roadmap and action plan to maximize my chances of finding ideal board opportunities that reflect my value and my values.

» I am continuously learning new skills and enhancing my abilities to ensure that I am the candidate of choice when applying to the boardroom.

» If I am offered a board role, I know exactly what questions to ask the board and myself to ensure I am making the right choice.

Cultivating your Five Cs

As you go through each of the five Cs above, write down your responses to the bullet point prompts, taking note of the aspects of each C that you already have and the aspects you still need to develop. This will help you identify how well-equipped you are and what gaps you'll need to focus on.

For example, you might be strong in credibility but lacking in community. If that's you, I'd recommend focusing more effort on networking, and of course, this book.

In the right combination, the five Cs give you all you need to be able to find and secure your ideal board role. But you also need a strategic roadmap and clear action plan to accelerate your journey to the right seat at the right table.

For this, you'll need the CONNECT method.

CHAPTER 4

IS GOVERNANCE TRAINING A MUST FOR DIRECTORS?

Before we build your roadmap and action plan using the CONNECT method, I first want to address one of the single most important questions I am asked by aspiring directors: Do you need a formal governance qualification to become a board director?

Most people aspiring to the boardroom believe that they need formal governance training or certification. While I don't want to denigrate governance training courses or those who have been through that process, I can tell you that it's frankly untrue that these are a prerequisite to landing a board role.

Before we talk about why governance training isn't strictly necessary for would-be directors, let's quickly bust a few myths around this belief.

First, boards value experience and variety in their directors over governance training. At the Future Directors Institute, our accelerator programs always include guest speakers from a variety of boards. Of these guests, fewer than half have formal governance training. Likewise, of the people who go through our programs and land a board role, even fewer have any formal governance training *before* they secure their first role. However, some do pursue formal training once they begin serving on their first board of directors.

Second, you don't need governance training to gain the basic financial and legal know-how to fulfill your responsibilities as a non-executive director. Although this knowledge is important, especially as it relates to your duties as a director, you can easily learn any initially important knowledge without expensive training. You can research this on your own, or you can ask someone with those specific skills to teach you. Deeper skills can and will be learned over time. This has been my experience and that of many in our community.

As a new director, it's highly unlikely you are being hired for your governance expertise. What's more important is your experience and how it relates to your contribution to the boardroom. What will distinguish you is how you work with others and your ability to prepare, question, challenge, and hold others to account. In short, you want to demonstrate the qualities that all Future Directors bring to a team.

Perhaps the reason that so many people seek governance training is because they believe the qualification will allow them to find board work easily. However, these training courses are not designed to offer guidance on how to land a director role. And, beyond some technical knowledge, they don't tell you how you can excel once you become a director.

The reason we've set up Future Directors programs the way we have is because we believe it's important to show you the practical steps to landing a great board role and the human (or soft) skills you'll need to succeed once you have it.

We encourage our alumni to include governance training in their board career plan. But, more importantly, we also encourage them to seek training or education in a wide range of areas in order to be better directors. For example, digital marketing, crisis management, cyber security, community engagement, product development, change management, and so on. As non-executive directors, you will be presented with ideas and strategies in these areas, and you need to be knowledgeable enough to assess the risks and opportunities for the company and its stakeholders. But do not think you need all of this *before* you enter the boardroom. While that may be highly desirable, it's more about what you learn and keep learning after you land that first role.

Again, this is not to say that governance training courses offer no value. They do, and most charge accordingly. But we believe the lessons they offer are best suited for people who are already on a board, because this type of technical training will be more practical and less theoretical once you're in a position where you can apply that training.

My advice is to understand exactly what governance training courses provide and to determine whether a particular course is necessary to help you to follow the path you have your heart set on. If, based on your research, you determine that governance training is an essential step for you, then by all means do it. But if you sign up for a governance training course—even a credible and reputable one—without knowing all the facts, then you may spend a large amount of money on something that doesn't offer much in return.

CHAPTER 5

THE *CONNECT* METHOD

Assuming I haven't scared you off, and you still feel the boardroom is for you, how do you go about getting your ideal role?

To help you do this, we developed CONNECT, Future Directors' unique seven-step framework for kick-starting or accelerating your journey to the boardroom and beyond. I have already discussed some elements of CONNECT, but they bear repeating to reinforce their importance to your journey.

There are three routes to getting a board role. The first is to apply to an advertised role. The second is to be invited to apply. The third is to be invited directly onto the board. What CONNECT is designed to do is help you circumvent the first route—although if you do take that route, you can be confident that you'll stand out from the crowd. Our ultimate goal for you is the third route: a direct invitation.

These are the seven steps to the CONNECT method:

Consider your commitment
Own your unique value
Nail your assets
Network your value
Execute the right plan
Conduct your due diligence
Thrive in the boardroom

It's important to note that, while Step 7 is technically about being *in* the boardroom rather than getting to it, knowing the best ways to thrive in the boardroom can help you to better define your unique value proposition. It's also important to note that, although it's best to follow the steps in sequence, you do not have to perfect each step before you move on to the next one. This is a journey, and even the most seasoned directors will define and refine the steps as they continue on their path.

Step 1: Consider Your Commitment

This goes back to the first of the five Cs: your why, what, when, and who. This is the foundation of your entire journey. It's what you can keep coming back to when things get tough.

Why do you want to be a board director? When do you want it? Who do you want to do it for? That focus, intent, and commitment will make this process easier, more efficient, and more productive.

Developing your commitment doesn't have to happen overnight. You can really put some thought into each of these aspects and keep this going while you move on to the next steps. For example, you don't have to know which board you want to be on before you continue. You should, however, know your motivations for being a board director and how much time you can commit to finding a role.

It's important to own your timeline, expectations, intent, and commitment. You should work toward whatever you want and do it in a way that makes sense for *you*, without being distracted by what others are doing. Your expectations might, however, change along the way. You might have been a little hasty in setting a short time horizon, or (like many aspiring directors) you may have underestimated how long it would take to find and secure a role.

I expect you have a day job. If so, it's crucial to figure out how you'll fit this new aspect of your professional life around what you do in that role or roles. These may all be tied together by a single theme. For example, you might work in the healthcare sector and want to sit on the board of a healthcare-related charity. These roles might also be completely separate. Again, this is personal to you; there is no right structure.

Getting on and serving on a board does take time and effort, so you also need to decide how much time you have to spare. Remember that the amount of time you'll have available to serve on a board is broadly equivalent to how much time you'll need to find that ideal board role. That said, the timeline is different for everyone, and you can take as long as you need for the process that we're going through in this book. The main variables are your starting point and how well positioned you are. That's why we believe it's never too early to start your research.

Actions to take at this stage

1. Be clear about your motivations for wanting to be a board director. If you are struggling with this, speak to others about their reasons. You want to be able to clearly articulate your "why" to others.

2. Set clear expectations. When do you want this? Is it months or years from now? How much time do you have to spare, and where does it rank on your list of personal and professional priorities? Start by devising a timeline and defining an amount of time (perhaps in number of hours per month) that you are willing to commit to finding your ideal role.

3. Understand what will be expected of you as a director. Make sure you've done ample research into what it means to be a board director, but don't rely on just one person for this. All board directors or governance commentators, myself included, have had their own unique experiences but with plenty of common elements.

4. Identify, as best as you can at this stage, where you wish to serve. Being a director is all about service. You might have a particular cause you want to support, a particular change you want to help bring about, or a

particular sector that is important to you. Don't worry if you don't have a specific focus yet. You can develop one as you go through CONNECT.

5. Write down your answers to the prompts above under the headings "why", "when", "what", and "who". Keep reviewing these as you go.

I can't stress enough that this step is foundational. Getting on a board will eventually come down to your commitment, so it's best to get started now in figuring out what motivates it.

ALAN JONES:
Defining His Commitment to the Ultimate Challenge

On the face of it, Alan might not seem like the type of person who would need help landing a board role. A successful and widely influential entrepreneur and angel investor, Alan was already on the boards of three different companies before we met.

While Alan had achieved what many would consider boardroom success, he hadn't yet managed to land a coveted director role for a top-listed company (his ideal role). As a highly motivated individual, this was primary among Alan's goals because of the influence that these large businesses have on our society. For Alan, it was not only a challenging objective to pursue; he also saw the personal, professional, and financial rewards that would come from such a role. But getting onto the board of one of these top companies is a very difficult task, even if you have the reputation of someone like Alan.

He decided to enlist outside help to develop a clear strategy for achieving his goal. After exploring the options for boardroom courses in Australia, Alan became frustrated by the narrowness of what they offered. He felt that many were overpriced or too conservative, and didn't reflect the diversity of industry that Alan believes in.

He then found Future Directors. With a philosophy and culture committed to developing the next generation of young directors and to changing the landscape of boardrooms for greater gender, culture, and age diversity, Future Directors was the perfect fit for Alan. Beyond what he got from our CONNECT method, he felt that he was part of a larger project that was disrupting the director space in an influential and positive way.

With the Future Directors team and their community of highly reputable board directors, Alan managed to assess what he could already offer to a listed company board as well as the skills and qualities that he needed to develop to make himself an even more attractive proposition to those companies.

Soon after graduating, Alan was offered a director role with a startup incubator that works with exceptional individuals from migrant and refugee backgrounds. Although this is not his ultimate goal, he embraced it as a rewarding opportunity, recognizing that the "who" of one's commitments can change. Now, once again, he's committed to fulfilling his ultimate challenge of landing a position on a big listed company.

Step 2: Own Your Unique Value

How do you stand out from the crowd? This second step of CONNECT is focused on crafting a compelling and powerful case for your contribution. What are your passions, skills, strengths, attributes, and experience? And how can they be used to tell a story about what you can and will contribute to your ideal boardroom?

It all comes down to how powerfully you can answer the question "Why you?" It is the most important part of the CONNECT strategy. We recommend that you focus the most time and effort on this. My job and a large part of what we do at Future Directors is to help you unlock your potential and articulate this unique value, because we know you're sitting on a mountain of good stuff. We call this your unique Boardroom Value Proposition (BVP).

The question "Why you?" has a flip side: "Why us?" When you're applying to and interviewing for a board, these are the questions they will want you to answer (perhaps not phrased in exactly this way). The right board role is about matching your unique value to a board's needs. Therefore, as you develop your BVP, it's important to ensure you make it flexible enough to tailor to your ideal board role.

You may not have substantial experience, but your unique combination of passions, skills, strengths, attributes, and experience is valuable to someone. You'll need to think beyond the default qualifications of your job title, career history, or education. It's more important to create a picture of the complete you, from a boardroom perspective: what you bring to the table that very few others have *and* that it is needed by that specific board.

The goal of this book is to give you insight into how you can unlock your unique BVP and articulate it in a way that is attractive to the people who will help you on your journey (your community) and also makes a compelling case to the boardroom for why they should hire you (your audience).

> **Tip:** *Stories that demonstrate your skills and experience are always worth telling. Don't focus on just your job title unless it demonstrates everything that you'd bring to the boardroom.*

So, how can you construct your unique BVP? What are the component parts? At Future Directors, we look at the following:

Motivations: What are your motivations for wanting to be a board director? Boards want to know your motivations and that you will be committed to them and their organization.

Passions and interests: What are your passions and interests, and what evidence do you have to support them? If you are struggling with defining your passions or even your interests, try these prompts:

> » What change do I think is needed in the world, and why is it needed? In this context, the world could mean your workplace, community, or indeed the entire planet. Think about what you actually want to change or improve.

> » What communities or stakeholders (i.e., employees, customers, society, and environment) do I want to impact, influence, and serve? Importantly, why do I want to serve them?

> » If you aren't sure about this, here are some deeper questions: What makes you angry? What brings you joy? What keeps you up at night?

Values: What are your values, and how do you demonstrate them?

Skills: What technical skills and experience do you possess, relating both to your profession and to governance?

Boards increasingly look for technical skills that fill a gap. They may be looking for legal, finance, marketing, fundraising, digital, or business expertise. You want to tick their boxes and demonstrate you have the right level of expertise to fill those gaps.

Strengths: What are your natural talents and core strengths, and what proof do you have of them? This includes technical skills but is focused more on human (soft) skills, or your characteristics and attributes. Boards are influential groups, and all their members bring something special to the table. We have found that focusing on what comes naturally is a good way to differentiate yourself from candidates who focus purely on their technical skills and job title. Most have the skills, but do they have your unique strengths?

Experience(s): What experiences have helped to shape and demonstrate all of the above? This is where storytelling is useful. Stories are powerful ways to articulate your BVP because they can connect people to you, especially if the audience has had similar experiences or has similar motivations, values, or passions.

You'll communicate your unique BVP by packaging these elements into a format that works for you. For example, it could be a few key stories, a series of bullet points under the heading "My Value to the Boardroom", or it could be a cover letter. Whatever you choose, it can continuously evolve and be flexible enough to be used in conversation, in an application, or while networking. It clearly states: "This is my contribution, this is my value, this is why you need me".

To consider this more concretely, let's use me as an example:

» (Motivation) I see the boardroom as a key conduit for change in the world. Decisions made in the boardroom have far-reaching impact and influence, and I am committed to working actively on boards that align with my passions and values. I support people and communities that need help accessing their potential, whether it's by providing the tools to make a positive impact or giving them the confidence to overcome (usually self-imposed) barriers.

» (Passion) I'm passionate about potential, so (not surprisingly) I focus on the future. More specifically, my interests lie in developing the potential of others: I help professionals to be the best version of themselves and to impact those around them in the same positive way.

» (Values) I value open-mindedness, justice, collaboration, and self-awareness above all else. I, therefore, seek a boardroom where these values are part of the culture.

» (Skills & Strengths) I am a natural communicator, coach, and facilitator, with the ability not just to create the strategies and tactical ideas but also to relate and structure the communication of these ideas to a diverse group. This lends itself well to the boardroom and the role of chair.

» (Evidence) I built the Future Directors community to do exactly this. My previous executive and non-executive experience and activities across the for-profit and nonprofit sectors are also evidence of my commitment.

» (Evidence) I am an international keynote speaker, published author, podcaster, and coach to Aspiring and Future Directors.

» (Aspirational) I'm also fascinated by how technology and our evolving understanding of neuroscience can assist leaders and groups to achieve an optimal level of performance and thus allow them to serve others to the best of their abilities.

There are many different ways you can actually bring your own story and unique value together, but the vital (and often overlooked) first step is being able to articulate your passions and motivations before your skills and strengths. In addition, the better you can express these in a way that matches what your audience wants to hear (i.e., in terms of the board's specific challenges, opportunities, and needs), the more powerfully your message will resonate. This is why it's important to be clear on who your audience will be.

Tip: *Speak and write in the present tense. Having aspirations for what you want to achieve is great, but for the boardroom, it is more effective to convey what you are doing already and that you want to do the same for them.*

Interestingly, it's easier to stand out from the crowd when you stand for something bigger than yourself. People can get behind a larger purpose, and having one will give your network the substance they can use in promoting you. This key insight will help you build a network of supporters, especially the ones who will talk about you and what you stand for. (More on that later.)

Actions to take at this stage

1. Write down all the elements of your unique BVP.

2. Speak to people you trust (family, friends, colleagues, and peers) about the skills, strengths, values, and attributes that they admire or value in you. If they have boardroom experience, ask them which of your qualities would make you a good board director. This might be a little uncomfortable, but you will gain powerful new insights into how others see you and what they value about you. This will only add to your unique BVP.

3. Use the power of storytelling. What are the stories that help you articulate your motivations, passions, skills, and strengths? You might need to commit a few stories to memory so you can draw on them in conversations and interviews, but make sure they're authentic and that you can tell them naturally. Those are the stories that your audience is going to find most engaging and powerful.

4. Practice, practice, practice! This is the only way to build confidence. If you can practice with others, that's even more powerful, as you'll get feedback on what is coming across well and what might not be working. The more confident you are in your content, the more impressively you will come across to your audience.

5. Do not wait for perfection. Your unique BVP is not static. It will be constantly evolving, so don't hold off on getting out there and speaking with others.

PARRYS RAINES:
A 22-Year-Old Pushing for a Sustainable Future

Parrys is a young woman who is already sitting on her first board, thanks to help from Future Directors. From an early age, she knew that she wanted to be in a position to make high-level decisions to enact change in an organization.

Eager to jump into a career as a director, Parrys immediately recognized what Future Directors and CONNECT could do for her. Unlike other programs she had researched, Future Directors was not focused solely on teaching the governance duties of a board director. Instead, the program was dedicated to helping participants discover their unique value proposition. For Parrys, the framework I've highlighted above was one of the most invaluable aspects of the course and helped her get her first board role because she could powerfully answer the question "Why you?"

One of Parrys' goals is to push sustainability and environmental consciousness onto board agendas. She deeply believes that if sustainability is ingrained in an organization from the top down, the business will experience a competitive advantage because it will show the public and consumers that the company cares about more than just profit. Like us, she believes that businesses wield tremendous influence on society and the future, more so than politicians, so pushing other companies and the public to be environmentally friendly can change the game dramatically.

In her first board position (with the Australian-based Future Business Council, a business membership and advocacy group that supports progressive businesses), Parrys has seen the huge impact that smaller organizations can have. For example, she is the CEO of the youth subset of a board called the Future Business Generation, consisting of young people between the ages of 18 and 28 who care about the future of the Australian economy and of work. By involving young people who are passionate about solving tomorrow's problems, the board is driving a message of intergenerational communication and equity.

Looking ahead, Parrys wants to pursue a board position at a larger organization and continues to draw on what she has learned. Parrys also hopes to empower and engage more young people to sit on boards, to push for diversity (especially regarding gender), and to take the lead in altering the fiduciary duties of directors, with respect to climate change. Parrys hopes her legacy will be as the director who supported board liability for Australian companies that fail to consider climate change risk and breach their duty of care for the future.

Step 3: Nail Your Assets

The first step focused on your motivations, where you want to be, when, and why. Next we started to develop your unique value proposition and discussed why you need to own it. Now we are looking at the assets you need to help build your credibility and networks and to prepare for the application process.

What do we mean by "assets"? Your assets are anything that helps to communicate your unique value. In this context, your main assets are your board CV (or resume) and your digital profile, best represented by LinkedIn.

You can also include other digital presences: the website for your business, a blog, or your profile on a more private social network. If you don't have a broader digital presence, or if you do and the content overlaps with your CV and LinkedIn profile, that's okay. Your CV and LinkedIn profile are, however, non-negotiables.

It's obvious why you need a great board CV (and possibly a cover letter): They are used by the majority of all recruiting boards and by recruitment companies who act on behalf of boards.

But why is your LinkedIn presence of equal importance? First, LinkedIn is *the* best and largest social network for professionals across the world. No matter who is leading the recruitment process, your LinkedIn profile will very likely be scrutinized. It will be compared to your board CV, and you'll be compared to other candidates based on your LinkedIn activity, so it's important to get it right. Next, LinkedIn is also a place to network with directors, influencers, and potential sponsors. We get into this in Step 4. Finally, while your board CV is specific and narrowly focused, LinkedIn allows you to present more content, evidence, and endorsements relating to your skills and experience. It's a powerful place to build your credibility.

The only case where you might not need these assets is if you are approached by a board to be a director. This is what the CONNECT method is designed to do: to help you become the object of direct approaches and to circumvent the usual application process. But there is no guarantee this will happen to you. Even if it does, it's likely that you'll still need at least a CV, so it never hurts to be prepared.

Let's go into those things in a bit more detail.

Your board CV: This is critically different from your normal CV, which you might have used in applying for a job. That's because of the significant differences between the role of a board director (mainly oversight) and the role of an employee, business owner, or executive (operational). Therefore, you'll want to highlight and demonstrate your non-executive abilities more than your executive abilities.

Some board roles, depending on the size of the organization (for example, a small under-resourced charity), may need you to perform some operational work, but the job of a board director does not typically involve operational duties. I know directors with specialist functions, such as accounting or public relations, who assist in that function as a professional volunteer. It's more necessity than responsibility.

This book won't give you a template for your board CV, but you can find plenty of those online, or you can learn about best practice once you become part of the Future Directors alumni.

What we will tell you here are some of the basic dos and don'ts of the CV, what to include, and what to exclude.

A great board CV does three things well. First, it demonstrates to the board that you are not a risk and can operate in their high-level environment. Boards are bearers of risk, so they want to ensure that their own members are not going to be a risk themselves.

The more boardroom experience you have, the less likely you'll be viewed as a risk because of any perceived lack of experience. However, even if you are experienced, you need to demonstrate that you can operate in that board's area of focus, structure, or style. You may have to demonstrate that you understand how a small nonprofit board functions if you've served only on the boards of large companies with substantial resources, or vice versa.

If you have no board experience, you might be thinking, "Won't I be a risk because of my lack of experience?" Remember, no one is born a board director, and everyone starts somewhere. There are plenty of ways you can demonstrate your relevant experience. For example:

» Have you ever been on a project team that had oversight rather than operational responsibilities?

» Have you been a mentor, advisor, or coach to other professionals or businesses? This one is useful, as it shows your ability to guide others.

» Have you served on a board subcommittee before?

» Have you been a skilled volunteer?

This last one is particularly important if your goal is a nonprofit or a volunteer board role because it's a demonstration of your commitment. The last two are also good routes to many of those boardrooms.

If you have demonstrated your abilities in these areas, however limited the scope, you'll be able to present yourself as a lesser risk. Remember, again, your lack of board experience might not be a factor given what else the board needs from you. It is worth repeating that everyone has to start somewhere, so do not be discouraged by limited board experience.

The second thing a great CV does is communicate that you'll be an asset to the board and the organization. This is where your unique BVP comes in: what you're going to bring to the board and what they need from a new director. Boards and recruiters might have to review numerous applications, so they will scan for keywords and phrases that match their expectations. The more your CV is tailored to their specific needs, the more clearly it will announce that you will be an asset.

Remember, your BVP is not just your technical skills and experience(s), but it also includes your motivations, core strengths, and attributes that would be an asset to any governance group. We delve more into this in Step 7.

The third and final thing a great board CV does is give the reviewer a clear handle on who you are, what you can do, and why they should choose you. In combination with your cover letter, your board CV should do this even with a quick skim.

Think about the key things you want the audience to remember about you. It's usually best to come up with about three core messages that are apparent throughout your application. It's okay to repeat yourself in some way if you think it's important enough. I do it in this book quite a few times!

As you put together your board CV, keep in mind these must-haves:

1. Your board CV is always tailored to the role you are applying for. Demonstrate your knowledge of the organization: Start with a template, but adjust the content to suit the board you're applying for (i.e., the sector, purpose, values, director needs, challenges, opportunities, and key stakeholders). You can learn this by reading their website and past annual reports and talking to key people in the organization.

2. Always prioritize your governance experience over your work experience. If you have none of the former, then focus on the parts of your experience that are relevant to the responsibilities of the boardroom.

3. Be honest and not necessarily modest about your achievements and experiences. One of the biggest mistakes people make is not selling themselves. This is especially true for outsiders like women and young people. If this is true for you, then seek help crafting a message that suits your humility.

4. Incorporate your unique value proposition throughout, but always ensure there is context. Using relevant keywords is fine, but don't use buzzwords unless they are universally understood or are used by the board you are applying to.

5. Demonstrate your ability to work on a diverse team. Remember, a board of directors is just a group of humans, each of whom should have an equal voice. It's a team effort, and you need to demonstrate how you can be an individual while part of the team.

6. Keep it relevant. Whatever you've done, make sure what you include is relevant to the role and the organization and conveys your unique BVP. If you are unsure, ask for a second opinion, perhaps from one of your new mentors.

7. Finally, be consistent with your LinkedIn profile. While your online profile might not be tailored, the dates and roles must line up; otherwise, it's a red flag that either a) you are massaging the truth or b) you pay little attention to detail. Neither of these is a good attribute for a director.

Digital profile and presence: LinkedIn is the biggest and most powerful online professional networking tool there is. Anybody you're going to be working for or working with is likely to be on the platform, and it's important that you use it effectively.

Your LinkedIn profile can support elements from your value proposition and any boardroom application. However, unlike your board CV, which is unique to the organization you're approaching, your LinkedIn profile is not tailored to the role but tailored to you and all the different parts of your professional life, not just the search for an ideal board role.

Your profile is an opportunity to include more detailed proof and testimonials to support your BVP. You can link published articles or other writing that demonstrates your thought leadership. It's likely that parts of your unique value will be relevant for board roles as well as for executive roles or your business. Your profile doesn't need to give the appearance that you are actively searching. If you're worried your employer might get the wrong impression, initiate a conversation with them—you might even find support for your board role search!

LinkedIn is also a powerful search tool, for you and for boards (and their agents). Boards can use it to search for candidates. They might also use it when conducting research on your application. If they Google you first to check your online presence, it's likely that your LinkedIn profile will be the first item returned in the search (unless you have a large online footprint, own a successful business, or have been published extensively). This is why you need a strong LinkedIn profile.

> **Tip:** *LinkedIn is not simply an employment profile. It's also a platform to build your personal brand and to connect with people inside and outside of your network.*

Make sure you have a professional headshot that reflects who you are. Think about what a selfie or a holiday snap says about you before you settle for one of those.

For your own research, search for board directors in your network or within an area of interest (see Step 4), or research key people at any organization you are seeking to join (see Step 5). You'll also find out if you're already connected to those people (as a 2nd-degree connection) through someone in your network (1st-degree connection).

Being introduced by someone who is a mutual connection is a powerful way to break through any potential barriers.

Now, here is a pet peeve related to LinkedIn etiquette: If you are going to approach someone directly on LinkedIn and send a connection request, please, PLEASE make sure you add a personal message. Be upfront about your intent, but remember that you want to cultivate the relationship. If you are seeking a potential mentor, ask for a meeting to discuss how you can learn from them (or words to that effect), instead of starting with a blunt request to be mentored. It may be an online conversation, but treat it as if you were face-to-face. Even if you know the person, add a message. It really does make a better impression and helps you build a supportive network.

Actions to take at this stage

1. Seek guidance on your board CV. Find templates online, or better still, ask to see the CV of someone you know and trust. It helps if they have been successful! If you have mentors, talk to them, too.

2. When it comes to your digital presence, take your time. It can seem like a massive challenge to develop your profile and your presence, but take it step by step. Start with the sections that would be easy to tackle, like beefing up your work history, education, and volunteering. Focus on sharing an interesting article with your audience on a regular basis. When you do, add your own comments so people know why you're sharing it and what you got from it.

3. When connecting with people on LinkedIn, don't forget to add a personal message. Would you hand your business card to someone on the street and walk away without saying a word? Even if it's someone you know, remember that it's a relationship, not just a connection.

JEREMY URBACH:
Positioned for Boardroom Success

Jeremy is a veteran Future Director and an early adopter of our methods. At the time we first met him, Jeremy had just started up his own company and recognized the need to discover more about the boardroom. Now, he is the director of his company—a boutique funds management and finance firm—as well as director and recently appointed treasurer of MND Victoria, an organization providing care and support for people living with motor neuron disease (MND).

MND had heavily affected Jeremy's family, and that was his motivation to help and get involved. Jeremy had always been interested in becoming a director and thought he could put his finance and strategy skills to use on a board related to MND. At the same time, he had been successfully starting his own company and was beginning to realize that there was no established method that teaches how a board operates effectively.

According to Jeremy, CONNECT gave him the insight and knowledge about how to market his skills and values and how to showcase his boardroom potential to organizations, especially online. We helped him answer these questions: Do I have what it takes? What could I bring to a board? How do I approach one? CONNECT also helped him to develop the confidence necessary to approach and explain to people, online as well as offline, why he'd be so beneficial for them.

It also taught Jeremy that you don't need to change your skills or attributes in order to be the perfect match for a board. He learned how to identify his strengths, how to identify a board best suited to him, and how to position himself in a way most advantageous to success.

With our help, Jeremy was also able to narrow the list of companies he wanted to target, which encouraged him to connect with them on LinkedIn. This newfound confidence and knowledge led to his success in achieving a board role at MND Victoria, where he can finally provide the help he has always wanted to give.

Step 4: Network Your Value

Building relationships and networking are essential to getting on a board. The process of board recruitment is still, by and large, a game of Who Do You Know. When a board is about to lose a director or has a gap, the directors sit around a table and brainstorm someone who would be a good fit from their collective network. The search ends when one of them announces, "I know someone. Let's talk to them and invite them onto the board". It seems unreal and it's not true everywhere, but tapping connections and network is still a significant part of the whole process.

This means you need to be in the right places and meeting the right people. Position yourself so that you are the one whose name is brought up at that table. Luckily, there are many different ways you can do this, to suit the introvert and extrovert alike. But you won't be able to sit back and wait for people to come to you.

The most important thing about networking your value is ensuring that people know who you are, what you want, why you want it, and who you're doing it for. The preceding steps are leading you to have the conversations that create connections and opportunities.

For the introverts, I have good news. Networking is more than attending an event with hundreds of people and giving your elevator pitch to countless strangers. Networking is also about having one-on-one meetings over coffee, phone calls, presenting to small groups of people, and connecting on social media and especially LinkedIn.

It doesn't have to be with just professional connections either. Talking to your friends and your family is, in essence, a form of networking. This builds a mutually supportive network of people—you'll help them, and they'll be able to help you.

It bears repeating that one of the benefits of a thoughtful and articulated unique value proposition is that it requires you to articulate the bigger picture (i.e., the communities and stakeholders you want to serve). This not only helps to distinguish you but also makes it far easier for somebody to support you. Think about it: Would you be more likely to support someone who is trying to address a very specific issue, such as protecting chimpanzees or LGBTQ+ rights, or someone who is chasing a board role to earn hundreds of thousands of dollars? If the specific issue is also of personal importance to them, that's even more helpful. If this were the case, wouldn't you talk to others and help that person move ahead? It's all about positioning yourself and (dare I say it?) your personal brand.

One of our program speakers once said, "Half of getting a board role is luck". We prodded, "What's the other half?" His answer: "Creating that luck." That is, you've got to get out there and network. You cannot assume people are going to find you, even if you have a stellar LinkedIn profile.

The importance of mentors and sponsors

Tip: *It's not just what you know or who you know that counts, it's also who knows you and what they say about you to others. That's influence!*

If you network your value well, you'll develop what we call sponsors. Sponsors are the people who offer up your name when opportunities come up. They know exactly what you want to do, who you want to do it for, and when you want to do it. If they know and can recall this information because they care about you and your success, they will make the connection for you. Having this backing creates a level of trust in the boardroom because someone they know can vouch for you.

Mentors, both informal and formal, are also vital members of your supportive community, and you are probably already aware of their importance. Make sure you also know that mentors help you in a different way than sponsors do: Not all mentors are sponsors, and not all sponsors are mentors. Some people aren't going to be in a position to introduce you to a board opening, but they may be able to help you develop the skills that will win you that board seat. For our purposes, there are three different types of mentors:

The Career Mentor: These are people who hold the executive leadership positions that you aspire to. They may be within your workplace, but they're preferably outside of it.

The Leadership Mentor: If you're thinking about a board career, you really should be presenting yourself as a leader. This mentor displays the attributes and leadership style that you want to emulate and can mentor you in that way of leading others.

The Board Mentor: Someone with boardroom experience who may be sitting on a board that you like or who is the type of board director you want to be.

These three types of mentors can be a single person, but it's best to have a number of formal and informal mentors. They don't have to have a label. Some are professional mentors that you may find within your organization or via a paid mentor platform. You may have even formalized that arrangement with someone. It doesn't matter. Find them in whatever way works for you.

Ideally, your mentors will offer practical advice and guidance on steps you need to take relative to the type of mentorship you seek from them. But more than that, great mentors will provide you with emotional and motivational support. They've been around the block: They've experienced the highs and lows and can talk you through the more difficult obstacles you're bound to encounter.

What stops people from finding mentors?

Self-doubt is the biggest obstacle that people face when considering whether to find a mentor. People become riddled with questions about the value they have to offer. They tell themselves that they don't deserve to have a mentor or haven't achieved enough to begin approaching potential mentors.

This is never the right attitude in any line of business, particularly when you're looking to build an important relationship.

The reality is if you have purpose and can articulate that purpose, then someone will want to support you. If you're experiencing problems with self-doubt when approaching potential mentors, then figure out what it is that you stand for and look for someone senior to you who shares similar values.

Don't make these mentee mistakes

Even once you've overcome your self-doubt and found a mentor, it's still your responsibility to be the proactive party in the relationship. Don't forget: Your mentor may have several other mentees besides you, so it's important that you take the initiative in cultivating the relationship.

Reach out with questions and concerns that you might have. Remember to keep your mentor in the loop with your progress and follow through on any connections, referrals, or general advice they offer you.

That said, it's important not to treat your mentor's advice as gospel. They're human, too, and not infallible. You're not obliged to execute their suggestions, so if something they say doesn't sit right with you, then seriously consider whether it's the right course of action. This is why having more than one mentor is so valuable. You can float different ideas around and gather a number of opinions on how to advance your career.

Knowing when to ask the right questions and using your intuition are important qualities for a board member to have, so you shouldn't be afraid to exercise these traits across all areas of your boardroom journey...even with your mentor.

Your network doesn't stop with mentors and sponsors (although they are critical elements of your strategy). Your network includes your supporters: the people who cheer you up and get you going, whose role is not to promote you or mentor you but to serve as an important support mechanism. These may be colleagues, friends, or peers. All of these people in your community can support you in your journey.

> **Tip:** *People are more likely to support and pro-mote you if you are making a stand for others.*

Actions to take at this stage

1. The key to networking your value is building relationships. Find out who you already know that could potentially help you. Look for board directors in your existing community, especially ones in your area of focus. Reach out to them for a chat and spend time getting to know them better. Be empathetic and responsive. Being busy is an easy excuse for inaction, and being invisible or unavailable will show others that you are not ready to be a director, even if you actually have the time.

2. Next, look at who else you want in your network. You can do this using what we call social capital mapping. This might not immediately produce specific names, but you can map the industry or cause that interests you (i.e., healthcare or animal welfare—the more specific the better), the types of board (i.e., nonprofit, startup, listed company, etc.), then perhaps a few organizations or companies, and finally, specific members of those boards. Then, get out there and find ways to talk to them. Do you know someone who can introduce you? Can you meet them at an event? Can you even approach them directly (via LinkedIn)? Even if the connection is online, make time to convert a message into an email, a phone call, or even a meeting. If you don't yet have specific directors or companies

on your map, talk to others in your network or focus area; they might be able to hook you up.

3. Take things one step at a time. It's easy to become overwhelmed with this part of the process. Just be patient. Set expectations and goals according to how much time you have and how quickly you want a board role. Everyone manages time and tasks differently. I use lists and block time in my diary to tackle specific projects. Do what is right for you. And if you don't know, there are more books on this than you've had hot dinners!

4. Keep an eye out for relationships that could develop into mentorships (remembering the three types). You can approach it formally through your employer or a paid service, but I think letting things be a bit more organic is better!

DANIELLE LEHRER:
Commercializing the Change Makers

After working in the financial and technology industries for well over 10 years, Danielle was savvy to the changes and issues the industry was facing—and she was able to see how those issues could be solved. The rapid pace of change was at odds with the ethos of the industry, whose larger, well-established companies were only too happy to remain stagnant, unwilling to accept any disruption to their status quo.

Danielle isn't one to sit idly by, and she felt the need to encourage acceptance of those changes. Like many innovators, Danielle believes that the entire world is on the brink of a revolution, and this belief encouraged her to seek a position on a board that would enable her to help her industry adapt.

However, Danielle faced the all-too-common problem that many aspiring board directors face: How could she go about actually doing this? Luckily, she came across one of my LinkedIn posts promoting Future Directors' work. Our method quickly gave her the ability to put a plan into action.

The benefits she has received from our program can be summed up in three words: discovery, focus, dedication. We helped her to attain a precise focus to her interests. Prior to Future Directors, Danielle had already successfully secured a number of board roles. However, she was unsure about what those roles truly meant to her and was unaware of how effective her impact could be. This is exactly what we helped her define. Now she has focused exactly where her passions lie and how she can make the greatest impact.

Thanks to our networking tactics, Danielle was able to seek out board mentors. Danielle had been a mentor for various startups but had not thought about having her own mentor to assist her in exploring and achieving a directorship. She's found this to be a priceless addition to her network.

Through Future Directors and our community, Danielle has also found like-minded board directors who want to approach changes to their industry with more enthusiasm. They're shifting the focus toward the endless benefits of change and away from a sense of threat to the usual state of affairs.

Step 5: Execute Your Plan

The previous four steps have prepared you to pursue a board role, but now we get to the step where you really begin to put that preparation to use and to pursue the role you want. Now, in doing this, you'll need to start building the action plan that will keep you moving toward your goal.

This step is about the best way to approach a board, proactively research your target organizations, and maximize your chances of getting an interview (if applicable) and securing a role. Before we get to that, however, let's briefly go over my thoughts on the best approach to developing your action plan. Then we'll get to how to secure a board role (which is what I promised in the title)!

Building an action plan

There are three key parts to a good plan:

1. Priorities and timing
2. Accountability
3. Execution

You have already set a timeline for this process in Step 1.

To establish your priorities, you'll refer back to the list of specific actions at the end of each preceding chapter (Steps 1 to 4). First, list the actions you want and need to take, and then prioritize them.

Here is one way that I prioritize actions (or projects). Write down on Post-It notes all the actions that you could take, one action per note. Then score each of these actions across a set of variables. For example:

» How long will it take?
» How much effort and/or money will be needed?
» What is the return on your investment in terms of your board journey?

Score each as you wish, say on a 10-point scale, and add up the total. Line them up from highest to lowest score, and see which ones have come out as priorities. Check this list to make sure it is logical, and then choose your priorities, allocate time, and set deadlines. For everything else, allocate less time or extended deadlines.

The next part is accountability. Self-management is great in theory, but we humans need systems of accountability to keep us honest. This doesn't necessarily mean a "boss", but it could mean a mentor, a peer, or a group of peers. Ideally, you'd find people who are on a similar journey so you can help each other keep on track. Make sure you're clear about the approach to accountability that works best for you. If you need to be ruled with an iron fist, establish that up front. If you need more forgiveness and compassion, then find someone or a group that will let you off the hook. There's no right answer. At the end of the day, it's about getting where you want to go in the time you have set to get there.

Finally, execution. It's no use setting goals, deadlines, and a system of accountability unless you get out there and do it. So, let's go over what you need to do.

Approaching the board

This may (or may not) surprise you, but most boards don't always know what they're looking for. If they do, they're not willing to put the time, effort, and potential expense into finding the right directors.

Although board roles can be recruited through many channels—an advertisement on job boards or social media, a search firm, or professional networks—it's the last one that is the most common. This is true regardless of the type of board and especially for smaller, volunteer boards, which are the majority. The most effective method for you to gain a director position, then, is to find ways to present yourself to the organizations doing the recruiting.

Tip: *Many boards don't go beyond a small network when looking for new directors. Get yourself into that network.*

Apart from networking your value, getting sponsored, or applying for advertised board roles, what else can you do to make the connections that will help you gain a seat in the boardroom?

Volunteer your time: If you are interested in a nonprofit, community, or school board, dedicate the hours you'd use for the search to do some skilled volunteering. Make sure it's skilled and not unskilled volunteering so it showcases your talents and commitment to some of the right people. This is a good way of getting on the "inside" so you are already known when they are recruiting for new board members. This could be serving on a committee or lending your expertise to a task or project, such as developing a fundraising strategy or helping with some legal work.

Be visible in the right places: If you know the board you want to be on, attend events relating to that organization or business, like the AGM (annual general meeting). Alternatively, find out where their board directors hang out. Perhaps one is speaking at an event. Don't be a stalker, but introduce yourself and chat about your aspirations. This is simply another form of networking. You could also become visible to these directors by writing an article or blog and approaching them for a quote. Similarly, if you aren't sure of the specific board you're interested in but do know the area of focus (for example, social justice or tech startups), be visible in those communities. Get involved in events and online chat groups. Find ways to demonstrate your value.

Search your LinkedIn 1st- and 2nd-degree connections: Given the staggering number of boards in the world, it's likely that people you know are board directors and you didn't even know it. Search LinkedIn for "board director" or "non-executive" and filter for 1st-degree connections. Then, reach out. Also, if you find some 2nd-degree connection names you want to meet, see if you know someone who can introduce you.

Search, search, search: There is no silver bullet for advertised board roles, no single website where they are all assembled waiting for you to find them. In each country, there are dozens of ways to find board roles. Some will be free to view, others behind a paywall (usually a member-based organization). Aside from director-focused groups such as NACD (National Association of Company Directors) in the US, AICD (Australian Institute of Company Directors) or IoD (Institute of Directors) in multiple countries, there are other community jobs boards for alumni groups and industry associations and publications. Your mentors and peers can also be sources of information for specific openings and ideas for how to find them.

Whatever happens, don't give up. Even if your approach is unsuccessful, each step in this process is a step forward. A rejection is not an occasion for blame, not even for blaming yourself. I've always found that a simple request for more information ("Thank you, do you know anyone else I should speak to?") is surprisingly effective and gives the person a chance to help you in a small way.

Preparation, preparation, preparation!

Given all the hard work you've done so far, make sure you don't waste that effort by being unprepared when you sit down in front of your ideal board, whether you apply to an advertised role, are approached to apply, or even approach a board opportunistically.

As you might have guessed by now, one of my favorite words is preparation. When applying to or meeting with directors from your ideal board, you'll need to do more extensive research and find the answers to the following questions:

» Who are the current directors? What are their skills and experience? Finding out about the directors should be relatively easy, as their website usually lists board members. If not, try LinkedIn.

» Who should I address my application to (if relevant)? Who will be on the interview committee?

» Do I know exactly what skills and experience they are looking for?

» What is their current business strategy? What are they trying to achieve? At what stage are they in this journey? What are the main challenges and opportunities for this organization? This is where you start seeing how you can add value: You might see the gaps in the boardroom or how you can enhance their collective abilities. What is their board structure? Do they have subcommittees? Could I get on one of those if I'm not successful at getting on the board? As we've discussed, subcommittees are a good way to get inside the board world.

Before we move forward, I want to talk about one member of our community, Naomi. She is a zealous sports fan, and her dream was to be on the board of her favorite team. Several months after joining our community, that team sacked their entire board and started the process of recruiting a new one.

Now, the team is in a predominantly male-dominated sport and its boards have been almost exclusively men, but this didn't deter Naomi. She applied for the board and was one of only a few women to be interviewed. She is in her 30s, and the board was not ready for such a young female director, so she was not successful. However, having done her preparation,

Naomi had a plan. She knew that the team's primary objective beyond winning games was to develop a broader fan base, especially kids. Naomi knew that when you talk about kids, the audience includes parents and especially mothers. The target market is, therefore, largely female. Undeterred by the interview rejection, Naomi set about helping to set up a group to engage and grow the female fan base for the team. It took a while, but now Naomi is in this group, helping to develop the team's corporate strategy. Needless to say, she is highly visible to the board. I suspect it won't be too long before they ask her to join them.

If you are struggling to find the answers to some of the questions I highlighted above, reach out to someone in the know. If you can speak to the recruiting team, CEO, or, better still, the board chair, you can find out information that might not have been stated in the advertisement and then tailor your application accordingly. In my experience, this also serves as a pre-interview and can help position you as a go-getter who is serious about due diligence. If you come to the conclusion at the end of the conversation that you are not the best candidate, it can also save you significant time and potential heartache.

If you do end up approaching a board directly and opportunistically, make sure you craft the perfect approach. If you take the approach that the board probably understands its gaps and needs but hasn't gotten around to looking for them, you can present yourself as the perfect "gap filler". By matching yourself to the organization, the board's gap, and the strategy that they are trying to achieve, you have gathered all the elements for winning a board role for yourself, without having to go through an application process with dozens, if not hundreds, of others.

The last point I want to make is relevant if your approach or application was unsuccessful. Good boards (although not all boards) are always developing a pipeline, or, to use a sports analogy, the bench. This is a group of candidates they can call upon to fill future gaps in the boardroom. If you approach a board and there is no open seat, or you're not the right fit right now, you could get onto their bench, assuming you impress them. That's a great outcome for you.

Actions to take at this stage

1. Develop your action plan, and prioritize those actions.

2. Establish a system of accountability, either with mentors, peers, or a group of like-minded people on a similar journey.

3. The best way to find the right opportunities is to learn how to sidestep the recruitment process and be invited onto a board. This is CONNECTing. But even if this happens, remember that preparation is everything. Every board is unique, with distinct strategies, risks, people, and structures. The more you know, the more closely you can tailor your approach and application.

4. Build a list of the organizations you are going to approach and the questions you need answered to maximize your chance of success.

JACQUIE FEGENT-MCGEACHIE:
Finding Confidence

Jacquie came to Future Directors with an impressive resume as a non-executive director for three years and a global executive for Kimberly-Clark. She was inspired to seek help for her next board role because of a specific ambition: to make a greater contribution to Sustainable Business Australia, an organization she cared deeply about. She also wanted to gain more experience in governance and to provide support and expertise in the corporate arena.

She had heard about us through the media and was impressed by the proposition of diversity across gender, age, and ethnicity on boards and the focus on individual influence and the dynamics of a boardroom. Although Jacquie had a fair amount of board experience before attending our program, her story demonstrates the value and insight that come from seeking help, whether it's from Future Directors or not.

Jacquie had been invited onto her previous boards, so she felt unsure of how to approach a board and express her desire to be on it. While she had set clear targets, she needed guidance on how to frame her pitch to Sustainable Business Australia to showcase her unique set of skills and values.

She also wanted to learn the best way to approach them to maximize her chances of success.

After working with us and using the CONNECT method, Jacquie gained greater confidence and motivation to actively pursue a seat on Sustainable Business Australia's board. She developed her pitch, approached them directly, and secured her seat at the table.

Step 6: Conduct Your Due Diligence

You've successfully followed the first five steps of CONNECT, found your ideal board role, nailed the interview, and secured an offer. That's fantastic—and it feels very flattering, especially if it's your first board role. But do you accept that board role straight away?

No. Take a breath, because this is one of the most important steps in becoming and being a board director: making the right choice.

The door is wide open for you. But, before you go through that door, you have to ask yourself and the board some strategic questions. Finding the right fit for your first board role (and for subsequent ones) is only going to enhance your reputation, your learning, and your skills—and will, therefore, extend and accelerate your career. It's vital that you conduct your due diligence and make sure the board is a good match for you before forging ahead.

Your efforts at due diligence will never be perfect. You're not going to know everything you need or want to know, but you can ensure you know enough to make the best decision.

Tip: *Your first board role can make or break your board career. Make sure it's a good fit for you and, just as importantly, for the rest of the board.*

There are three aspects to your due diligence.

The first part is asking yourself the right questions: Is this the board role that I really want? Is it the right time to join them? Are we a good fit? Am I going to enjoy it? If you're getting on a board because you want to make a difference, as I'm sure most of you are, then you're going to be passionate about the organization and what it does. But this doesn't automatically mean it's the right board for you to join. Try to put this passion to one side and think about your choice rationally.

The next part is asking some questions of the board or your connections on the board, (if you have them). You want to find out what their expectations are of you and your fellow directors (assuming this was not discussed with you earlier): How much time do they expect you to commit? What commitments should you expect beyond your participation in board meetings and subcommittees? What is the board's structure, and what are its values (if you don't already know)? Does the board have an open and collaborative environment, or is the board political and hierarchical?

There is no right answer to these questions, and there is no "best" board. It's up to you to judge whether this is the board role that *you* should accept. For example, if the board is slightly political, but you thrive in political environments, then perfect—go for it. This is why it's so important to really own your value proposition and to understand yourself and your commitment. There is no one-size-fits-all.

The last part of your due diligence is to collect as many of the board's documents, minutes, policies, and procedures as you can, so you can understand as much as possible about the organization. Do they operate by the book, in terms of basic financial requirements or in terms of director's insurance? Do they have a code of conduct for directors? What's the expense policy? You can even ask for copies of past meeting minutes, to see how meetings are run and how decisions are made and recorded. How long are board directors expected to be on the board? Is there a term limit? Can directors be fired?

If you don't get the materials you ask for, this could be a red flag. The organization might have something to hide. If there's no explanation for why they cannot give you all the documents, I caution you to be at least a little suspicious.

However, it's also possible that the delay is entirely innocent. Perhaps they've never been asked these questions before. A number of people in the Future Directors community have come across this: The boards they were considering were new to due diligence but were so impressed with this careful approach that they built new induction processes around them.

Careful due diligence can also enhance your reputation even before you start your board tenure. Some alumni have found that their intelligent and insightful questions as part of the due diligence process—that is, thinking like a good board director—made their transition onto the board easier.

Assuming you complete this step to everyone's satisfaction, congratulations, you can take your seat at the right table!

Actions to take at this stage

1. Remember, preparation is everything. Every board is unique with its own strategies, risks, people, and structures. The more you know about each of these, the better chance you'll have of not only being chosen but making the right decision to accept or decline the role.

2. Write down a list of the questions you need to ask yourself and the board. Seek advice from your mentor or, better yet, get involved in Future Directors!

3. Keep learning, even when you think you've made it. Never assume you know everything you need to know—that's impossible.

DANIELLE BEEMSTERBOER:
The Importance of Due Diligence

Danielle had wanted to join a board for a long time. She'd always seen it as a great way to be involved with, and give back to, her local community. She is passionate about disability and women's rights, and she knew that, with her dedication and skill set, she'd be able to make meaningful contributions to both those areas.

Prior to coming across Future Directors, Danielle had applied for two boards. She didn't make it to the interview stage, a failure that she attributed to lacking the right knowledge and required experience. The CONNECT process filled those gaps for her, but they had nothing to do with governance experience or her expertise. The key knowledge that Danielle gained was how to articulate a value proposition that would best showcase her unique worth and governance credibility.

The main insight for Danielle was the importance of due diligence in securing the right board role. This last aspect was a crucial factor in a tricky decision Danielle had to make shortly after finishing the program. She had found her ideal board and been invited to apply for a director position. However, after reviewing the organization's annual reports, she found that the board's poor decisions had left their finances in a mess. She decided it was in her best interest to turn down the board role.

Aside from the importance of due diligence, Danielle learned what it takes to progress from simply applying for board roles to receiving invitations to interview and even further to advancing through interview rounds. Thanks to our personal touch, Danielle was able to give both her resume and her LinkedIn profile an overhaul, making them better suited to the roles she was after. The program also allowed her to hone her interview skills, which helped her feel confident and prepared for the interviews that have occurred since.

Critical mistakes people make when looking for a board role

Before we move on to our final step, I want to take you quickly through some common mistakes people can make going through this process.

Having the wrong mindset (part 1): In most countries and across most board types, the average age of directors is about 60. Traditional thinking about board careers holds that you only start once you've had a successful and long executive career, perhaps in the C-suite or as a business owner. So, you'd be forgiven for thinking that you need to have been a CEO and at least in your mid-40s before thinking about the boardroom.

As we know, these are myths. But these myths could be enough to scare off any outsider. You might be doubting yourself and telling yourself that it's not for you, you're too young and too inexperienced, or that you don't have the right skills.

This is the wrong mindset to have. We've shown you throughout this book what is possible if you use our CONNECT method. We have also given you case studies to inspire you with typical examples of people who have already done this successfully.

There are a growing number of traditionally "outsider" directors on the boards of nonprofits, startups, and private and publicly listed companies (although they are still relatively few in the largest publicly listed companies). The traditions of board recruitment are also changing fast, as boards recognize that diversity is crucial to future success. New directors bring different perspectives on an ever-changing world and are digitally savvy. They are also representative of what is now the largest segment of the workforce and soon to be the largest investor base as they inherit assets worth trillions.

Remember: We all had to start somewhere, and you are never too young to start a board career.

Having the wrong mindset (part 2): Sometimes the critical mistake is not a lack of confidence but overconfidence. As an aspiring director, you'll quickly discover that getting a board role is not easy. Being a director is hard work and a serious commitment (although many on the inside are not as committed as they could or should be). Attaining that coveted ideal board role can be just as hard, unless you put in the right effort.

I've met plenty of senior professionals who fail to land their first non-executive board role even with a relatively distinguished executive career and some technical governance training. These individuals often suffer from a sense of entitlement or the wrong expectations. I say the same thing to them that I say to you...

You need to take action, follow the CONNECT method, and make things happen for yourself. You might have to apply for a few positions, and you might even be rejected. However, just like *anything* in life, the more effort you put in, using the best strategy for you, the more you're likely to get out of it.

Not having clarity and focus: Do you know yet which type of boards you want to be on and why? Do you know what makes you stand out from a crowded pool of candidates? Do you know how to avoid being lumped in with that crowd? Do you have a long list of people willing to vouch for how brilliant you'd be as a board director?

If you want to become a director (at any age), you have to sell yourself. But in order to sell yourself effectively, everything about you must shout credibility, contribution, and value. The more focused you are on what you want and what you have to offer, the more powerfully you can communicate this in a way that is attractive to boards.

Not developing a supportive network: Your fourth mistake is not building a supportive network. The key word here is "supportive". It's relatively easy to build a network, whether online or offline, but you'll need to take the right approach to build one with people who actually want to promote you to others. A what-can-you-do-for-me attitude might get you somewhere but not far. You may get short-term favors and connections, but these people are not going to support you all the way up.

The way to build relationships and networks is to think long term, "What can I do for that person?" and "How can I actually help them with what they need?" More importantly, a supportive network is crucial when things aren't going very well. You want to be surrounded by people who are there for you when it all hits the fan. This is a key role that a truly supportive network will play.

So get out there, talk to, meet, and share with your network—and not just the people you already know. Some of the most successful graduates of our programs have met their mentors or sponsors by approaching people they didn't know before.

Not doing your due diligence: Even the most seasoned director can get carried away and forget to do their due diligence. I hear about it all the time.

Only say "yes" if the board fits your values. Make sure the boardroom is not a mess of politics and hidden agendas—unless you've done the self-examination to know that this is exactly the type of place where you'll thrive.

Step 7: Thrive in the Boardroom

You've been offered a board role, you've conducted your due diligence, and you've accepted your ideal board role—congratulations! This is huge news, and you should celebrate the achievement. I hope we helped in some way.

We've now reached the final step of the CONNECT method, and this is all about who you are in the boardroom.

Our mission at Future Directors is to develop a new generation of exceptional directors. We want you to be the best director you possibly can be. We want you to *thrive* in the boardroom. This will not happen from your very first meeting, but you should learn where you are heading and get there as quickly as you can.

Thriving means turning up and being intentional about every interaction you have with the board. Sitting passively during board meetings will not help you thrive: You'll need to prepare for every meeting. And you'll have to build relationships with your fellow directors and management as well as other stakeholders, staff, investors, or big donors, and the community at large.

By doing what you need to do to thrive, you'll be a more effective director. You'll maximize your impact and your influence. You'll also accelerate your boardroom career by gaining confidence in yourself and a sterling reputation with others. Once you are on the inside, it's far easier to find more board roles—even paid ones. Once you begin to thrive, you'll also be seen as attractive boardroom talent, and other boards may start recruiting you.

We are going to discuss more about thriving in the boardroom in the next few chapters, but I wanted to leave you with this thought. You are now an insider. You have a seat at a table, or maybe many tables. Don't keep it to yourself. A great director will actively encourage others to get involved in and enter the boardroom. You can do this in so many ways. But one of the best is to point them in the direction of Future Directors. Pass it on!

PART III

You Made It. What Do You Do Now?

While this book is focused on finding and securing your ideal board role (and I'm confident that if you follow the method you'll join hundreds of outsiders who can now call themselves insiders), I can't leave you to attend your first board meetings ill-equipped to handle the pressures and challenges of becoming an influential director.

Therefore, this part of the book is designed to help you once you've gotten a seat at the table. It covers:

» Things that no one (but I) will tell you about being in the boardroom

» The main challenges faced by new directors—and how to overcome them

» Key attributes and character traits of effective and influential board directors

Tip: *The single most important thing to remember about the boardroom is that it's just a group of human beings. All directors have their own views, egos, backgrounds, stories, strengths, and weaknesses. The more you understand this and know how to elicit the best out of every individual on the board (including yourself), the more successful and influential you will be.*

CHAPTER 6:

WHAT NO ONE TELLS YOU ABOUT BEING IN THE BOARDROOM

As stated from the outset, stepping into a boardroom can be a pretty intimidating experience. For many, it's daunting just to think about trying to get there, let alone being there. How should you behave? What exactly is expected of you? What are the processes and protocols you need to follow?

Chances are, if you ask around you'll be bombarded with too much information—some of it useful and some of it less so—on what directorship is like and what you should be doing.

In this chapter, I'm going to discuss the things that no one else will tell you about being in the boardroom. And this is based on my own experience and that of the hundreds of people Future Directors Institute has worked with. I'll also pass along some tips on how to succeed and caveats of what to avoid at all costs.

No one has a clue what's going on: This first one might sound like an embellished truth, but trust me when I say that no one in a boardroom is as knowledgeable as they might seem. I can tell you any number of anecdotes from experienced directors about how surprised they've been at their fellow directors' lack of knowledge—and sometimes even their own!

Particularly as a new director, it can be tempting to believe you're the only one who does not know exactly what's going on. However, you'll quickly realize that your fellow directors are simply human. They all have their own issues, blind spots, and hang-ups that they have to navigate.

You've been invited into that boardroom for a reason: They believe that you have something to offer. You have skill sets and qualities that others in the room don't. You've jumped through enough hoops and proved that you deserve to be there. You're just as prepared as anyone else.

It's okay to speak up on the first day: One of the major mistakes that directors often make in the boardroom is not asking questions or not being willing to voice a challenge. Newly appointed directors sometimes assume that, because they're surrounded by experienced people, their input is not required or perhaps not even expected.

Don't fall into this trap. Your job is to contribute your unique services and expertise.

Offer substance, not speculation: While I firmly believe that you should make your voice heard, it's important that the input you offer is valuable and moves the conversation forward.

Don't put forth speculative opinions just for the sake of it. You don't want a reputation as someone who is insubstantial.

You should feel comfortable relying on the skills and experiences that have gotten you this far. Ask questions that you feel need to be asked, and offer suggestions that you know would be valuable to the boardroom as a whole.

The most important thing about being on a board is relationships: One of the key points we stress at Future Directors is that preparation equals influence. When it comes to preparing yourself to enter the boardroom, there's far more involved than reading and understanding the board papers. Instead, you need to know about your fellow board members, the managers, and the stakeholders of the company. Find out about their motivations, challenges, wants, and needs. ·

Some people are surprised by the importance of interpersonal relationships in the boardroom. But if you do a little research into the people you'll be interacting with and use a little emotional intelligence, you'll be even more effective when you walk through the door.

The chair is the most important person in the room: It's important to develop a relationship with everyone in the boardroom, but there's one relationship that holds more weight than any other for you as a director—the chair. This person has the power to give you a voice, influence, or esteem.

When building relationships in the boardroom, you should start with this person, especially on larger boards where it's harder to have your voice heard.

CHAPTER 7:

COMMON CHALLENGES FACED BY NEW DIRECTORS

Achieving your goal of gaining the right seat at the right table is not the end of your journey. Once you've secured your ideal board role, you will probably be presented with challenges and obstacles.

Below are three of the most common challenges faced by new directors, as well as suggestions for how best to overcome them so you can accelerate your transition from board amateur to board influencer.

Figuring out exactly which skills you'll need

One of the most common questions we find new directors asking is "What kind of skills will I actually need?" This stems from the common belief that before you can join a board, you must have already maximized your skill development. This simply isn't true.

You don't need to be at your professional peak to be a great board director. In fact, many effective directors are at the beginning of their career. Remember the case study of Parrys Raines. She is in her early 20s and is already an influential board member. As a new director, you aren't required to have an extensive list of skills and specialist achievements. Often, all you need is an open mind and an eagerness to learn.

Of course, it is very helpful to have a basic idea of the type of skills you'll need. It's not entirely necessary, however, to begin working on them right away. You can build these skills throughout your board career, once you have a more profound understanding of the organization's structure as well as the roles and responsibilities of its board directors.

For example, the most common skills-based question we get is about finance knowledge: "Can I become a board director if I cannot fully understand financial statements?" Again, it depends on the type of organization and what they need from you. While it is your responsibility to be able to govern to the best of your abilities without relying solely on other directors' skills, the reality is that you cannot know everything—you just need to know enough. You might not need this knowledge immediately, but your aim should be to acquire it quickly.

Whenever you develop the necessary skills, your network and connections will be critical. Make sure to surround yourself with mentors, coaches, and others who can assist you in expanding your skills. Enlist their help to get a solid understanding of the structure of the organization, the roles and responsibilities of the directors on the board, and the specific duties you will have to undertake.

Finding your voice and becoming influential

It can be uncomfortable when you feel that you lack presence and influence because you're the newbie in a situation. It's understandable if you feel apprehension and nervousness when you join a board. Indeed, these feelings can continue well into a board career. You are not alone, though, and the most confident-sounding person can be hiding a mess of nerves.

Fortunately, there are really simple and effective ways of overcoming these feelings. First, remember that you belong there. It sounds stupidly simple, because it is. You have been accepted onto the board, and that gives you an equal voice with everyone in the room regardless of tenure.

Next—and it needs repeating again and again because it is so important—be as prepared as possible. This includes getting to know your fellow directors before your first meeting and continuing to build those relationships. You'll find that your first board meeting will feel a lot less nerve-racking than it might otherwise because you've already met a few (if not all) of your colleagues.

The more you **know your audience**, the more influential and helpful you can be, on both an individual and an organizational level. To learn about your audience on a larger scale, reach out to key company stakeholders such as management, major donors, suppliers, and important customers. You should ensure that doing so doesn't break any protocols, so check with the chair first. Depending on the company's culture, the board and chair may or may not encourage that sort of transparency and integration. If you encounter resistance, it might help to remind the chair that the more you speak to and understand the different stakeholders, the better you can serve and govern them in your board role.

When to talk and when to listen

Even after you've overcome the first two challenges, it's important to know when your input is (and is not) needed. This is not about having the confidence to speak up in the first place. It's about speaking only when you have real value to add.

Knowing when to speak can come from your preparation. Read the necessary papers and conduct all research beforehand so you know what will be discussed. Understand your own point of view and why you have that point of view. With this preparation, you will be able to join in with the proper relevancy and knowledge.

Not only will prior preparation enable you to mix well with your fellow directors, it'll also get *your ideas* heard faster and to better effect. Demonstrating that you're well informed on the topics you're speaking about will encourage your colleagues to listen to you and respect your opinions. You can further extend your influence by talking to directors outside of board meetings too. Establish yourself as an authority in whatever areas you're passionate about, and people will pay attention.

However, no board is going to appreciate the input of someone who is clearly talking just to be heard or who is repeating what's already been discussed by others. So pick your battles, do your research beforehand, and really think about the value of what you're trying to say. If you are invited to contribute but don't have anything new to say, just say so. You'll earn more respect for moving things along and not wasting precious time.

If you're struggling with knowing how to approach your new position, it can help to consider the board as a family. You have to work on building relationships and trust, getting to know them, and even dealing with any potential dysfunction (because some families are like that!). Remember that you have been recruited because they have seen something in you. If your confidence falters, remind yourself that you have a right to be there, no matter whether you've been with them for five minutes or five years.

The most important thing is to be consistent and patient. Take one step at a time and you will find your stride. Work on building a great support network of mentors and teachers around you, and lean on these people for opinions and advice when you're feeling lost. No one has achieved success alone—all of the most successful people have had supporters around them the whole time.

So, in summary:

» You deserve to be there. They appointed you.

» Say it as you see it. Why hold back?

» However, don't speak unless you have something valuable to add.

» Practice being courageous and confident. Take acting classes!

» Be prepared, draw together different issues, and arrive with questions.

» Try testing your ideas in subcommittees or with individual directors (even your mentors).

» Keep developing your skills in key areas and become known as a trusted source.

» Learn how to interact with different types of people and get the most out of the relationships. Remember, the board is just a group of humans.

CHAPTER 8

ATTRIBUTES OF AN EFFECTIVE AND INFLUENTIAL DIRECTOR

Being a board director requires a certain amount of common sense, intelligence, and compassion. If you're an aspiring board director, you might be wondering whether you'll have what it takes. As long as you have these attributes (or are willing to learn them), you can become an effective and influential board director, or what we have called a Future Director.

Emotional intelligence

Emotional intelligence (measured by emotional intelligence quotient, or EQ) is more important than intellectual intelligence (measured by intelligence quotient, or IQ). EQ is defined as the ability to monitor both your own and other people's emotions, to discriminate between different emotions and label them appropriately, and to use emotional information to guide your own thinking and behavior.

I also like to think it includes the ability to be self-aware about your biases, strengths, and weaknesses—and to be receptive to new ideas. The best boards are diverse, and respectfully so. Diversity isn't effective if it's met with conflict and aggression from those with opposing ideas. While it can often be difficult to put your personal opinions aside, being a successful board director includes keeping an open mind to that diversity and being vulnerable enough to admit when your mind is being changed.

These are all vital in the diverse boardroom. When you know yourself and how you interact and connect with others, you're more able to remain calm in stressful situations and to make better decisions, especially as part of a collective.

Commitment

The ability to commit is one of the key qualities of an effective board director. Often, people don't realize how time-consuming sitting on a board can be. It's not just a matter of turning up once a month for a few hours. There are committee meetings, trainings, strategy and planning days, and company events that you'll need to take into consideration.

You may also be involved in fundraising events, networking, and acting as an ambassador for the organization. You will also be building sustainable relationships, not just with your fellow board directors but with the stakeholders, investors, donors, and the management team. This workload can be manageable, even if you have a day job. But you have to first decide whether you're committed, because it will soon show if you're not.

Equanimity

The ability to remain calm and composed, even under stressful or difficult circumstances, is a beneficial attribute because tensions can become high in the boardroom and arguments can erupt. The ability to remain calm, no matter how fractious the boardroom gets, will land you in good stead.

Keeping your cool when everyone else is losing theirs will also help you make better decisions. This might not be possible for everybody, but it will help you thrive. Listen to your fellow board directors, even during the most heated arguments (which won't be a problem if you have that aforementioned emotional intelligence).

The work of the boardroom will not always be smooth sailing, and you'll probably experience ongoing crises that will test you and your fellow board members. An emergency of global scale might arise, and some directors might panic. Or there might be external pressure to fire a controversial CEO, or perhaps a volatile board director unleashes a nasty tirade. If you are the one who remains grounded when all the others are losing their cool, you'll be perceived as more effective and reliable.

Preparedness

I will continue to drill into you the need for preparation! If you're heading into a board meeting with no idea of what's to come, it will never look good—regardless of whether it's your first board meeting or your fiftieth.

Being prepared involves not just the mechanics of serving on a board but also the people you're serving with. By deeply considering the issues, you'll persuade your fellow directors with your thorough approach. By researching your audiences and their histories, you'll be able to appeal to their motivations and navigate sensitive topics, whether you're in a conversation with fellow directors or with stakeholder groups. Preparation *is* influence.

Mindful impact

The boardroom, when run correctly, can be the point of origin for changes with a substantial societal impact. This powerful influence can be either positive or negative, and successful board directors will always be mindful of the impact their decisions can make.

Thinking on both the micro and macro levels can help when considering the possible ripple effect of decisions made by your board. Ask yourself about the impact on the stakeholders, investors, donors, and the community, and take that into account with each decision.

Bravery

Part of being an effective board director is being courageous, speaking up, and standing up for what you believe in. You might find this hard to do if you are more prone to being passive. But change won't emerge from your passivity. If you aren't brave enough to speak up in the boardroom, especially about the issues that motivated you to join the board in the first place, how will you effect change? If you want to make an impact, you have to make some waves.

Bravery in the boardroom means understanding what important questions need to be asked—and having the smarts to know when you should ask them. Challenging assumptions—both your and those of your fellow directors—and asking the right questions can help keep your board on topic and on the right path.

Dispassionate passion

Passion is key to boardroom success. But being able to remain dispassionate about those passions is equally important. Often, your board might come up against highly charged topics. It's great to have strong feelings and beliefs, but keep in mind that remaining coldly logical about them is the only way you will be able to make better, more effective decisions.

Discernment

A great director is comfortable saying no, even to good ideas. This can be hard for some people, but you will come to learn this skill throughout your career. Being able to prioritize the best ideas while rejecting others (no matter how great they may seem) will only benefit your board. Using your resources based on these priorities ensures that you always tackle what's most important.

If you've read through this list and are feeling downcast because you feel you don't have one or more of these attributes, don't despair. These are all learned behaviors that you can achieve over time. To become a successful board director, you need to learn and grow as you go—and you'll have a more satisfying board career the more you learn early on.

Ultimately, all of these characteristics are about increasing your influence and impact as a leader. If you think about why you started this process in the first place and what got you to this point, you'll return to the difference you wanted to make and the change you wanted to see in your community, your country, and the world. Cultivating these traits in yourself is what will make you as effective, influential, and impactful as possible while working with your board to realize these changes.

GAYA BYRNE:
Diversity Advocate and Boardroom Change Agent

Gaya has a strong belief in the value of diversity, and she recognizes that it's a necessity in all organizations, especially at the highest decision-making levels. Gaya currently works as a strategy consultant at one of the world's largest telecommunications companies, and she's all too aware that it's important to have strong voices and leaders at the helm of any organization.

Still only 30, Gaya is an influential non-executive director at a prestigious, royally appointed, and well-financed women's hospital foundation in Australia, where she raises funds for research projects and infrastructure. Despite being the youngest director by several decades, she is already influencing innovative thinking about fundraising and organizational strategy, the very skills that the board needed and why they hired her.

But Gaya also knows that if the decision makers don't have the same perspectives as the audience they're trying to serve, they won't have the profound, necessary impact that is required when trying to make change. This realization and desire to make change inspired Gaya to get into the boardroom.

Gaya credits her strong value proposition, developed with Future Directors, as a key part in her getting the role. Gaya had done a lot of volunteering in the past, and she believed she had different, relevant perspectives that she could bring to a board. While the program gave Gaya the necessary skills and confidence to properly articulate the value she could bring to a board and how to get what she wanted, it also gave her the blueprint she'd need to fulfill her role as an influential director. For example, it taught her the skills and attributes she'd have to acquire, the best people to network with, the confidence in finding a mentor, and the hands-on practical experience to do it all.

ARE YOU REALLY CUT OUT TO BE A DIRECTOR?

There are millions of businesses, nonprofits, schools, startups, governments, and community groups in the world. Almost every single one has a governing body, a board of directors, trustees, governors, or members. And new ones are established every day. Therefore, by extension, there are millions of potential board roles out there.

Many incumbent directors bring great value and undoubtedly deserve their seat at the table. Unfortunately, many on the inside do not deserve their seat, and many on the outside, who do deserve that seat, find it hard to get one.

Just because you think you can be a director doesn't mean you should be one.

Now that you've read this book and (hopefully) feel more confident to move forward in your journey from being an outsider to a boardroom insider, I now present your final checklist.

All potential directors need to ask themselves this one question before beginning their pursuit of a boardroom career: "Am I really director material?"

There is no simple way of telling whether you will make the cut. But to help you answer this simple, yet direct, question, I've broken it down into seven questions:

Please don't think you must answer every question "correctly" to make it as a board director. In fact, you don't have to answer any of them at all. There is no one way to measure your readiness. If you are leaning toward the "correct" answers on most of the questions below, you're going to be at an advantage when it comes to being an effective director.

Good luck!

Question 1: Do you prefer to work alone or with others?

If you answered the latter (with others), then congratulations, the boardroom could be for you. There is a bit of solo work in being a director (for example, that critical preparation) but most of it is about working as a collective. And don't expect the team environment to be smooth sailing all the time. Hopefully, the board will bring diverse views and skills, and this could lead to some healthy debates. But I hope it also brings an inclusive environment. To quote management expert and author Ken Blanchard: "None of us is as smart as all of us".

Question 2: Do you have time to spare?

Every board is different. But for a non-executive role, assume a commitment of five hours per month for an advisory board role up to several days per week for a role with a complex corporation that includes sitting on multiple subcommittees and further duties. With most boards, the average commitment is about 20 hours per month. But I stress again that every board has different needs and expectations. If you can spare this time, you are ready.

Question 3: Do you like to learn?

We live in nonlinear and dynamic times with increasing pressures from many more quarters. As a board director, you cannot remain static if you want to remain relevant. You need to add to your existing skills to enhance the value that you bring to the board and to keep pace with the organization's opportunities and challenges.

This goes beyond financial, legal, or even fundraising skills. Increasingly, you need to grasp customer-centric product and service design, the latest technology impacting your company (and soon your job), evolving risk and transparency issues including business ethics and workplace culture, marketing and human resources trends, new reporting requirements, and global economic and social issues (such as climate change).

If you are a learner, the boardroom is a good place for you.

Question 4: Are you used to getting your own way?

Yes? Then get out of the way. The boardroom is not the place for dictators. It is the place for influencers who work as part of a team. You'll need to put your ego to one side and be open to having your mind changed or going with a majority view. Your role is to act in the best interests of the organization and its stakeholders, not to dogmatically stick to your personal agenda. There are too many egos in boardrooms. We don't need any more.

Question 5: Do you struggle with difficult decisions?

As a director, the buck stops with you and the board. You must be willing to make tough choices and decisions that may significantly affect people, sometimes not always positively, or as positively as they'd like.

However, this is a bit of a trick question. If your answer is "no", then perhaps you do not care enough to be a director. If it's "yes", then perhaps you don't have the steel to make the tough choices you'll have to make. Boards often have to weigh competing priorities and stakeholders. You cannot please everyone all the time when acting in the organization's best interests.

The ideal answer is "Yes, I struggle but not for long". This means you can balance mental toughness and empathy to handle the burden of making decisions that will affect many people. Balance is key. Try not to dwell on decisions; you probably won't have the time.

Question 6: Do you prefer to listen or talk?

Listening is important as a director. You'll need to listen to management and their needs, the views of your fellow directors, and the needs and concerns of your stakeholders. Yes, listening and analyzing what you hear is vital. But so is talking.

Having a view, when it's qualified, is your job. You are not meant to be passive all the time. Asking the right questions at the right time, being considerate, being helpful, and being challenging yet supportive is the role of a director. If you need a refresher, go back to Chapter 8.

If you can "communicate with two ears and one mouth", then you'll make a great board director.

Question 7: Do you take pleasure in helping others?

Finally, this is a simple one. "Yes!" is the right answer. Being a board director is all about serving others. You offer your time and your skills, often solely for the gratification that comes from service. There's often no financial reward, although it's a bonus if you're compensated for your contribution.

Remember, though, it's not only others who gain from you being a director. You do too. You'll learn new skills that will make you a better director, a better employee, indeed a better human being. You'll meet new and interesting people. And who knows where that will lead? You might get paid for some roles. But even if you don't, you'll probably earn more in other non-director roles because of the new skills and relationships you've gained. You'll certainly be trusted to take on more responsibility.

How did you do?

As stated at the beginning, there is no right and wrong way to be a director. There *are* rules that govern the job and the board, and there are expectations that will vary from board to board. But you are on your own journey and in control of your own journey. It might take weeks, months, maybe even years to find and secure your ideal board role. But keep going, keep in action, and keep looking for help and inspiration from your community.

AFTERWORD

I hope that, having read my book, you feel confident to be able to find and secure your ideal board role, whether it's your first one or one among many. Either way, I hope this book will help you expand your horizons and accelerate your influence in the boardroom. Whoever you are, I wish you the very best of luck—although, as you now know, you'll be creating your own luck and will be on your way to a board role before you know it.

Wherever you end up, I hope that you'll always remember that as a board director, your job is to serve others first and yourself second. Do not forget that your individual and collective decisions have far-reaching implications and you'll be faced with difficult choices. This is where the diversity offered by you, the outsider, can and will add to the robustness of a group discussion: You'll bring new and unique insights. And ultimately, the group's decision will likely be more informed and better executed. Diversity is a source of resilience, innovation, strength, and assurance.

But beware: Diversity for diversity's sake is wasted. You need to embrace a culture of inclusion. Again, this is where the outsider (who becomes an insider) can add significant value and be influential.

Like the Future Director, a role I hope you're already aspiring to, you will motivate others, and in time, they will look to you for guidance. You will bring a collaborative mindset and help establish or enhance the inclusive culture that leads to better decision making, better policy, better risk management, and better strategy.

These challenges and opportunities are part of the extremely rewarding experience of being a board director— just ask any of the hundreds of directors we've helped to achieve their goals.

Finally, if you need help or a confidence boost and want the support of a growing community of inspiring and purposeful directors around the world, then the Future Directors Institute (and I) are here for you.

Now go make the world a better place—from inside and outside the boardroom! I look forward to seeing you out there.

GOVERNANCE TRAINING FOR NEXT-GEN LEADERS

The program that transforms you from aspiring director into a boardroom influencer

With well over 400 graduates, our award-winning program has helps hundreds of aspiring and developing directors to find and secure their ideal board roles. The program leaves you with a well-defined boardroom value proposition, deeper understanding of the role and responsibilities of being a director and how you can become an influence in the boardroom.

Check it out and you will see why 100% of participants now recommend the program.

www.futuredirectors.com

WE ALL NEED A LITTLE EXTRA HELP TO GET STARTED....

Whilst Paul's main business is group training programs for aspiring and developing directors, he also works with a select number of individual leaders, directors and boards. Paul is a successful and influential board director and he's passionate about empowering, educating and enhancing future leaders and future boards - those making a real difference in the world.

As a coach and mentor, he works with people and teams from all over the world. If you want to work one on one with him, your leadership can't help but grow dramatically.

To find out more about being coached or advised by Paul, shoot him an email at hello@futuredirectors.com

NOT QUITE READY TO COMMIT TO FUTURE DIRECTORS? TRY OUR FREE DIRECTOR DIAGNOSTIC.

Our proprietary Director Diagnostic tool is a way for you to analyse how equipped you are to move forward and what your expectations should be if you want to include non-executive director roles in your leadership journey.

COMMITMENT	Know what you want and when you want it
CONTRIBUTION	Articulate what value you would bring to the boardroom
CREDIBILITY	Think, look and act like a future board director
COMMUNITY	Who knows you and what do they say about you
CONFIDENCE	Maximise your chance of securing your 'ideal' board role

Using the 5 C's (remember those?) and in less than 5 minutes, we'll tell you how ready and able you are to get that right seat at the right table and recommend steps for you to move forward.

It's a great compliment to this book and is COMPLETELY FREE.

If you want to take the next step, check out the diagnostic used by over 1,200 professionals at www.futuredirectors.com/diagnostic

PAUL SMITH HAS DELIVERED OVER 100 PRESENTATIONS, WORKSHOPS AND KEYNOTES ACROSS 5 CONTINENTS. ALL DESIGNED TO EMPOWRR AND EDUCATE HIS AUDIENCE ABOUT THE POWER OF GOOD GOVERNANCE.

(Paul interviewing Dr Jane Goodall at Macquarie University)

Clearly Paul knows a thing or two about leadership and the world of boardroom governance. He speaks on a range of topics from generational diversity and inclusive decision-making to finding your voice in the boardroom and the future of governance, his particular favorite topic.

Paul's style is engaging, visionary and often tangential—he's got plenty of memorable stories of the good, the bad and the ugly of the boardroom to share. Paul can cover a range of topics that are transformational, relevant and customised to suit your audience.

To find out more about getting Paul to talk at your next event, please shoot him an email at hello@futuredirectors.com or connect via LinkedIn (search ' Future Paul Smith')

WANT TO KNOW WHAT THE FUTURE HOLDS FOR BOARDS AND THEIR DIRECTORS?

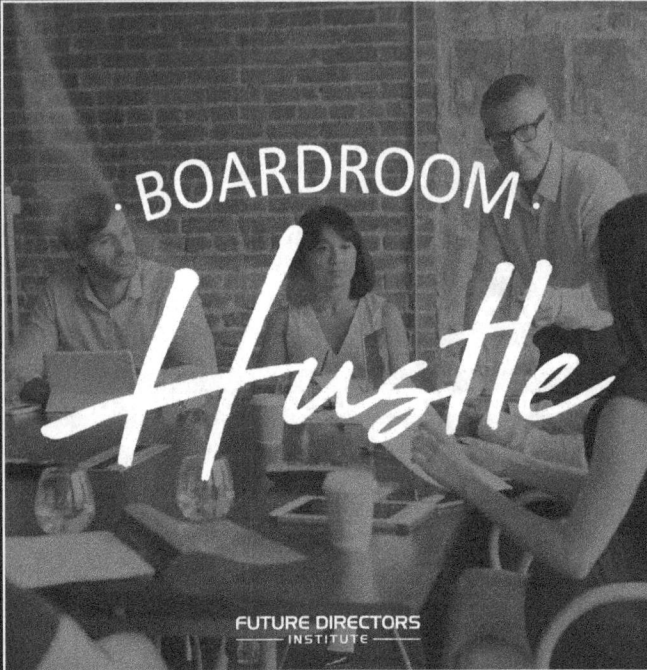

BOARDROOM Hustle

FUTURE DIRECTORS
— INSTITUTE —

Check out Paul's podcast show "Boardroom Hustle". Alongside co-host Anna Byrne (partner at NeuroPower), each episode delves deeply into the world of governance, technology, social dynamics and human performance.

Paul and Anna always have a special guest and they come from all over the world. They may be working on some of the most cutting-edge aspects of future governance but your hosts always look to find practical ways for listeners to take meaningful actions today.

CHECK OUT THE BOARDROOM HUSTLE PODCAST ON ITUNES, SPOTIFY OR YOUR FAVOURITE PODCAST PLATFORM.

ABOUT THE AUTHOR

Paul likes to do things a little differently and is unquestionably on a mission to help others fulfill their potential for positive change. He is a corporate executive turned social entrepreneur and non-executive director. He has been a board director and chair for almost a decade and has trained hundreds of boards and directors from Australia and New Zealand to the USA and Asia.

He's an international keynote speaker, podcaster, coach, and governance advisor. While he's proud of his work and accomplishments, what he values more is family, friends, and community.

Paul is a natural communicator, strategic thinker, and lover of ideas. He's also what you'd call a boardroom futurist—someone obsessed with the future of governance and the composition and mechanics of directors and boards. Despite having had dozens of book ideas in the past decade, this is Paul's debut book. It brings together what he's learned—from his own experience and the experience of hundreds of directors across the world—about getting into your ideal boardroom and making a bigger difference in the world.

His company, Future Directors Institute, helps individuals, directors, and boardrooms around the globe fulfill their potential, do things differently, and create a better world from inside and outside the boardroom.

You can connect with Paul on LinkedIn and Twitter at *futurepaulsmith*.

www.ingramcontent.com/pod-product-compliance
Lightning Source LLC
Chambersburg PA
CBHW071659210326
41597CB00017B/2246